Women Advocates of Reproductive Rights

Women Advocates of Reproductive Rights

Eleven Who Led the Struggle in the United States and Great Britain

by
MOIRA DAVISON REYNOLDS

McFarland & Company, Inc., Publishers
Jefferson, North Carolina, and London

British Library Cataloguing-in-Publication data are available

Library of Congress Cataloguing-in-Publication Data

Reynolds, Moira Davison.
    Women advocates of reproductive rights : eleven who led the
struggle in the United States and Great Britain / by Moira Davison
Reynolds.
      p. cm.
    Includes bibliographical references and index.
    ISBN 0-89950-940-1 (lib. bdg. : 50# alk. paper) ∞
    1. Birth control—Great Britain—History. 2. Birth control—
United States—History. 3. Pro-choice movement—Great Britain—
History. 4. Pro-choice movement—United States—History. 5. Sex
instruction—Great Britain—History. 6. Sex instruction—United
States—History. 7. Birth control—Biography. 8. Women social
reformers—Biography. I. Title.
HQ766.5.G7R48 1994
363.9'6'0922—dc20   93-41201
                                                      CIP

Manufactured in the United States of America

McFarland & Company, Inc., Publishers
 Box 611, Jefferson, North Carolina 28640

To Davison women of two generations—
my sisters Betty, Brenda, and Jean;
also my nieces Sharon, Dana, Patricia, and Jean Marie

Table of Contents

List of Illustrations

Preface and Acknowledgments

This book is about British and American women who spearheaded the movement to win reproductive rights for women and freedom with regard to the related issue of sexuality education. Many women were involved in the struggle; I selected as the subjects eleven who held particular interest for me. As with my two previous books about women, this one is intended for the general reader of either gender.

Despite great progress in the field of contraception, there are still, regrettably, many unwanted pregnancies that end in legal abortion. Since abortion is a controversial issue, I feel obligated to state my personal stand: I strongly favor retaining the right to early abortion, a right guaranteed by the 1973 Supreme Court decision known as *Roe vs. Wade*. At the same time, I respect other views and have tried to be evenhanded in presenting the subject.

My thanks go again to the staffs of the Peter White Public Library in Marquette, the Lydia M. Olson Library of Northern Michigan University, and the Superiorland Library Cooperative. Joanne Whitley of the latter continues to locate all sorts of materials that are difficult to find, and for this I applaud her. I have a special word of appreciation for Lea Menko and Lynn Paulsen, who translated some of Dr. Aletta Jacobs's writings from the original Dutch.

Moira Davison Reynolds
Marquette, Michigan
Fall 1993

ix

Zeal is blind when it encroaches on the rights of others.
—American proverb

I found myself obligated to inform the women who wished
not to become pregnant on social, moral or medical
grounds that I had an anti-conception product available.
—Aletta Jacobs, 1854–1929

Introduction

The history of contraception has been a history of both
methods and of attitudes.
— Clive Wood and Beryl Suitters,
The Fight for Acceptance, 1973

Efforts to control reproduction go back to antiquity. Significant progress came, however, only in the nineteenth century, when technical advances such as the vulcanization of rubber were conducive to the movement. Before considering the history of birth control, it will be useful to examine some attitudes common in the United States and Great Britain during much of the Victorian Age.

Women did little about emancipating themselves while sheer survival remained a real aspect of their lives. As living conditions improved, their first steps towards that goal were in the field of education. Advanced education for women was possible at a few institutions and the situation gradually improved, but the choices were still very limited. Low-paying jobs as teachers, domestics, and factory operatives working under deplorable conditions were sometimes available, but it was assumed that marriage was the lot of every woman.

Once married, a woman had virtually no rights; for centuries the law held that she could own no property in her own name. If she worked—which was unusual—her earnings were legally her husband's. Wife beating was permitted and divorce was most difficult to obtain. If a divorce was granted, the husband, not the

1

wife, usually obtained custody of the children. (And women were regarded as incubators for numerous children.)

The Reverend John E. Todd of Massachusetts (1800–1873) published some 15 books as well as pamphlets and sermons. A popular author, some of his writings point to accepted beliefs of the day. For instance, he claimed that masturbation would "enervate the physical and mental powers of man." His views on birth control are clear: "The great object of the marriage institution—the rich blessing from Eden—is not that the husband may live in legal fornication, and the wife in legal prostitution, but fulfil the first great command in the Bible." He was referring to Genesis 1:28, which orders, "Be fruitful, and multiply."

Since prostitution was common during the nineteenth century, sexually transmitted disease, then referred to as venereal disease, presented a problem. Syphilis and gonorrhea occurred frequently; chancroid less often. The causative organism of syphilis was not discovered until 1905, and the first really effective treatment of the disease was not available until five years later. Syphilis could ultimately cause insanity in adults; congenital syphilis could also have serious consequences. The organism responsible for gonorrhea was not known until 1879; effective therapy came much later and the disease left many women sterile. The bacterium that caused chancroid was found in 1890; satisfactory treatment came only with the antibiotic era.

A British woman named Josephine Butler became a champion of prostitutes. In combatting the Contagious Diseases Acts that regulated the activities of prostitutes, Butler drew attention to the era's different standards applied to husbands and wives in matters of sexual conduct and to the unequal treatment of prostitutes and their clients. (The former, if infected, were penalized, while the latter, if infected, were free to spread disease.) She also pointed out that in France and Prussia licensing laws produced no significant diminution in the incidence of venereal disease, and argued that hard economic facts drove many young girls into prostitution.

This is the story of several British and American women who were involved in winning reproductive rights and the right to education about sexuality; it is an account of the difficulties they encountered and of the problems that persist today.

One was Fanny Wright, a Scot by birth and a reformer with diverse interests. Associated with the socialist group in New Harmony, Indiana, she advocated, among other rights, equality for women, free love, and birth control. There was little support for such ideas during the pre–Victorian age when she was active. Nevertheless, her espousal of such radical ideas was a beginning.

Annie Besant was another British reformer who preached freethinking and socialism. In 1877 she was tried for immorality for her part in reprinting an old pamphlet on birth control. She was acquitted—albeit on a technicality—an event that indicates some progress during the Victorian Age.

Emma Goldman was a Lithuanian immigrant to America who devoted her adult life to the promotion of anarchism. An outstanding lecturer, she stressed the rights of the individual. Most of the rights she advocated incensed her contemporaries; she was arrested in 1916 because of her stance on birth control. Although birth control was only one of her concerns, Emma Goldman's tactics apparently made a deep impression on Margaret Sanger.

Unlike the first three women, Margaret Sanger was born in the United States. She embraced most of their beliefs but differed from them in one important respect: she directed her energy to one aim—that of making contraception available to all, here and abroad, who wanted it (and to all whom she could persuade to use it). She was subjected to arrest and imprisonment and once evaded the law by fleeing to England, but her accomplishments far exceeded those of her predecessors.

In 1921 an English paleobotanist named Marie Stopes became Britain's foremost lay advocate of birth control. Emphasizing sex education, her work ultimately led to widespread support, including that of the Church of England, which originally opposed her efforts.

Mary Dennett, an American, was a leading light in a voluntary parenthood league; she too focused on sex education. Even though her activities took place well into the twentieth century, she was convicted for using the mail to distribute such literature.

Mary Calderone was an American physician who wrote an important book on contraceptive practice. It was published in 1964, the same year she founded the Sex Information and Education Council of the United States (SIECUS), the organization that became her continuing interest.

Under the influence of the aging Margaret Sanger, Katharine Dexter McCormick helped to finance the research and development of the birth control pill under the leadership of scientist Gregory Pincus. This pill became available in the 1960s.

In 1966 noted feminist Betty Friedan founded the National Organization for Women (NOW), which advocated access to contraception and the legalization of abortion. Some seven years later, the United States Supreme Court made abortion legal, subject to restrictions involving health.

The 27-year-old lawyer who successfully argued *Roe v. Wade* before the Supreme Court was Sarah Weddington. Although at the time she lacked legal experience, she was singularly fitted to handle the case; she had herself had an illegal abortion.

Since Weddington's victory, there has been continuous opposition to liberal abortion laws, much of it arising from religious and moral scruples. Advances in neonatology and research on birth defects have also influenced the thinking of the prolife movement. Abortion has become a divisive issue as well as a political one and remains a significant problem facing the United States in the closing years of the twentieth century.

Virginia Johnson, with a background in psychology and human sexuality, represents women who have more recently contributed to the struggle for reproductive rights through enlightened thinking about sexual matters. She was coauthor of the bestseller *Human Sexual Response* in 1966 and coauthor of *Human Sexual Inadequacy* in 1970. In 1988 she and her coworkers issued a warning and a plea for responsibility with *Crisis: Heterosexual Behavior in the Age of AIDS*.

Collectively and with the help of countless others, male and female, these women did change prevailing attitudes about human sexuality and contraception, but they were less successful with the abortion issue.

Chapter 1

Frances Wright

The mind has no sex but what habit and education give
it, and I who was thrown in infancy upon the world like
a wreck upon the waters have learned as well to struggle
with the elements as any male child.
—Frances Wright, 1822

A publication entitled *Views of Society and Manners in America* appeared in England in 1821; its author, Frances Wright, was identified only as "an Englishwoman." The book was well received by many readers, including two men who would have an important impact on the author.

The first was Jeremy Bentham, then in his seventies, the British political theorist who pressed for prison reform, codification of the laws, and extension of the vote. His *Principles of Morals and Legislation,* written in 1789, held that the object of law is to achieve the "greatest happiness of the greatest number." (This is in contrast to egoism, which emphasizes self-interest.) Bentham had considerable influence on the birth control movement. Through him Frances Wright would meet such people as James Mill, the philosopher and economist, and Joseph Hume, also a philosopher.

The second reader who would influence Wright was the Marquis de La Fayette, the French general and political leader who had helped obtain an American victory in the War of Independence. He was also the creator of the French tricolor flag familiar to us today. His connections would open American doors to the "Englishwoman" writer.

5

Frances Wright, better known as Fanny, was born on September 7, 1795, in Dundee, Scotland. Her father was James Wright, a well-educated merchant who was known to have liberal views. Her mother, Camilla Campbell, was a member of the British aristocracy. Both parents died before Wright was three. Separated from a brother and a younger sister who was also named Camilla, Franny Wright was sent to London to live with her maternal grandfather, a major general in the Royal Marines, and her 18-year-old aunt, who was also named Frances.

Wright was eight when her uncle was killed in an accident. A wealthy man, he had left one half of his estate to Frances Campbell and the other half to Wright and her sister. This meant that Wright was eventually financially independent, a matter of some significance when appraising her actions. Frances Campbell soon moved to a beautiful home in Devonshire with Wright, and Camilla joined the family there. Wright had no affection for her aunt and later referred to the sisters' exposure to "violence and insult" at her hands. Although Wright had an unhappy relationship with this woman, she was brought up in comparative luxury. She appears to have been a precocious and sensitive child who benefited greatly from the excellent education she received.

In 1813 the Wright girls went to Glasgow to live with relatives of their father. James Mylne, their great-uncle, was a professor at Glasgow University. He and his wife, Agnes, were liberals, as were friends and relatives that frequented their home. The atmosphere was a striking contrast to that experienced by Wright under the Campbells. At an early age, she had become aware of the marked differences that existed between rich and poor. Her grandfather seemed indifferent to the plight of those less privileged than himself, but in the Mylne home she sensed a social consciousness in tune with her own.

The period following the Napoleonic Wars brought unemployment and high prices. Radical reformers came forth, but their efforts were met with the enactment of restrictive laws. As Wright observed with concern the mounting disparities between classes, she developed almost a compulsion to visit the United States, a land she believed to be "inhabited by free men." (How she reconciled this with the existence of slavery is hard to understand.)

The year 1818 saw Wright, then almost 23, and her sister, Camilla, sail from Liverpool to New York, a journey that kept them at sea for 30 days. Robina Craig Millar, the widow of a relative and a favorite of Fanny Wright, had once lived in the United States. Her letters of introduction helped the sisters meet interesting and influential persons, and Wright wrote Millar long letters that would be the basis of *Views*. After spending eight months in New York, the young women traveled to Montreal, Philadelphia, and Washington, as well as to Maryland and Virginia. Their stay in this country lasted almost two years.

Views painted an overall uncritical, enthusiastic, rosy picture of the United States, no doubt colored by the fact that Wright was disillusioned by what she had seen previously, as well as what she witnessed after her return to England. She did note, however, that "to inhale the impure breath of [slavery's] pestilence in the free winds of America is odious beyond all that the imagination can conceive." The book attracted considerable attention, but today it is much less known than Frances Trollope's *The Domestic Manners of the Americans,* published a decade later. Alexis de Tocqueville's *Democracy in America* (1835) is much more familiar than either woman's work. Nevertheless, *Views* established Wright as an author. (Her play *Altorf* had been produced earlier in New York, but only for two nights.)

Views impressed Bentham so much that he invited Wright to visit him. For some years they discussed mutual interests in person or by letter. As noted, their friendship afforded Wright opportunities to meet liberal persons who broadened her intellectual horizons.

Her book also enabled Wright to meet La Fayette in France, a country she began to visit frequently. She was among the many friends and relatives invited to his château. At the time, she was close to her twenty-sixth birthday, while he was in his sixties and a widower. Correspondence between them shows a mutual attraction, but the nature of their relationship is not clear. Obviously the general's admiration for the principles upon which the United States was founded struck a responsive chord in Wright. It is also pertinent that he had joined the Société des Amis des Noirs (Society of the Friends of the Blacks), founded in 1788.

In 1824, La Fayette paid another of his triumphal postwar visits to America. Fanny and Camilla Wright wanted to join him, but to prevent gossip, they arrived in New York a month after he did. Traveling extensively—often on horseback—they were welcomed in various eastern cities by La Fayette's friends. They met personages such as John Quincy Adams and James Madison, and they observed Congress in session. Much of the time La Fayette was not with them, but they managed to make contact with him at various points.

Fanny Wright soon withdrew the focus of her attention from the general and became intensely interested in how slavery could be eliminated. While visiting Jefferson at Monticello, she discussed with him the institution of slavery. Contrary to his thinking, she saw amalgamation of the two races as a logical consequence of abolition. The American Colonization Society helped free blacks find new homes in Haiti or Africa, but Wright was initially against this policy.

Intending to see slavery at its worst, Wright started for New Orleans in March 1885, accompanied by Camilla. On their way to the Mississippi, they visited an experimental community at Harmonie, Indiana. Dedicated to cooperative rather than competitive labor, this was a Utopian religious village, originally founded in 1815 for Germans by George Rapp. When Rapp moved his followers back to Economie, Pennsylvania, in 1825, the Indiana village was sold to Robert Owen. Wright first saw Harmonie when it was in a period of transition. She did not fail, however, to note its prosperity and undoubtedly gave consideration to the idea that the united labor of slaves could be equally successful.

Soon after their arrival in New Orleans, the Wrights were reunited with La Fayette, who was also visiting the city. Here Fanny Wright saw much evidence of miscegenation and became convinced that in time to come, that city's population would be composed largely of persons of mixed blood.

On the trip north from New Orleans, the women stopped again at Robert Owen's Wabash River village, later known as New Harmony. Owen had been a successful cotton manufacturer in Manchester, England. Interested in the welfare of his workers, he set up a model community in New Lanark, Scotland. At New

Harmony he was conducting an experiment in cooperative living to show that poverty could be abolished through shared labor and collective ownership.

When La Fayette departed for France in July 1825, the sisters were not with him. They became American citizens, presumably intending to stay. And by October of that year, the *New Harmony Gazette* had published Fanny Wright's *A Plan for the Gradual Abolition of Slavery in the United States without Danger of Loss to Citizens of the South.*

Influenced by what she had seen in the Indiana community, Wright envisaged slaves working tracts of land provided by Congress, with some of the profits from their labor eventually paying for their freedom. She estimated that 50 to 100 workers would be needed for each community; under favorable conditions, the length of servitude would be about five years. Each community would also include whites interested in the cause. She intended to have the community's children—black and white—educated together through the Lancasterian system (whereby more advanced students, under direction from the teacher, were used to instruct other pupils). Although Wright upheld miscegenation and disliked colonization in theory, her plan anticipated that most freed slaves would be removed to non–United States territory. She did suggest that this might not always be necessary, however. Wright apparently regarded her scheme as a practical means of ridding this country of an institution she deplored. Since profit was essential, hardworking individuals of both races were needed.

Wright relied on advice from a man named George Flower, who had a good knowledge of farming and was also sensitive to the plight of slaves. An immigrant from England, Flower had settled in Albion, Illinois, where Fanny and Camilla Wright stayed with him and his wife. In December 1825, Fanny Wright, with Flower's approval, bought 320 acres in the Wolf River area near what is now Memphis, Tennessee, to try out her proposed plan. (She would later add to this acreage.) She hoped that if she could demonstrate success, other states would provide for similar communities, so that in time slavery would disappear.

Although Wright's plan was publicized, it evoked little response in the form of live bodies to carry on the work. Wright had actually purchased some slaves for Nashoba, as the community was named. At the beginning of March 1826, when it opened, there were 18 blacks, including several children of various ages. Camilla and the Flowers had arrived from Albion. George Flower, who became Fanny Wright's partner, would supervise the slaves as well as manage a farm, but he and his family would live in Memphis. James Richardson, originally from Scotland, became a kind of business manager. Conditions were very primitive, with only two cabins built and very little land cleared.

It was soon evident that the profits from agriculture, if they ever materialized, would be a long time in coming. The land was not productive, and malaria was a problem. With their slave background, the blacks were not as motivated to work as were the Germans that Wright had seen at Rapp's village, and communal organization at Nashoba was not successful. Wright and Flower seem to have treated the slaves in a compassionate, if paternalistic, manner. They were both in close touch with Owen's group, and there is no doubt that many of New Harmony's goals became part of Nashoba. Especially controversial was Owen's opposition to organized religion, to marriage, and to the holding of private property. Although such ideas matched Wright's own, they were too radical for the times, and Owen's New Harmony experiment was abandoned after two years.

Nashoba was a failure also. A few months after it began, Wright became extremely ill from some febrile disease. Her recovery was so slow that in June 1827 she left for France in search of a cure. She was accompanied by Robert Dale Owen, a son of Robert Owen. Wright had been impressed with this young man, six years her junior, since knowing him at New Harmony. This was an especially unfortunate time for her to leave Nashoba, however, because George Flower and his family had abandoned the project. His replacement was a man from New Harmony named Richesson Whitby, who lacked Flower's ability. Thus Nashoba was left without strong leadership.

The daily events at Nashoba were carefully logged. During Wright's absence, James Richardson provided *The Genius of Universal Emancipation,* Benjamin Lundy's Baltimore publication, with excerpts from his log. One passage in particular caused a furor: Richardson reported that he had begun to live with a young woman. Regarded as a free black, she was the daughter of a mulatto woman hired to be in charge of the children at the experimental community. Elsewhere Richardson wrote that it was the consensus at Nashoba that the proper basis of sexual intercourse was the unconstrained and unrestrained choice of both parties. So here in print was an affirmation of New Harmony's free love. There was also the implication that miscegenation was acceptable.

Wright was in France making a gradual recovery when she learned of the adverse publicity. Although her course disturbed friends whose opinion she valued, she did not publicly refute Richardson's remarks. Instead, she concentrated on recruiting people to join the community. (Robert Dale Owen was doing this on his own.) When she returned to Nashoba at the beginning of 1828, however, she had only one candidate—Frances Trollope. The mother of novelist Anthony Trollope, she was later known for her authorship of *American Manners*. Trollope brought with her a party of six.

By this time Richardson had left, as had his paramour. Robert Dale Owen's search for recruits had been unsuccessful. Camilla had married Whitby—this despite Nashoba's commitment to free love. The couple departed for New Harmony after a few months. Trollope and her retinue did not stay: appalled at the conditions, she took up residence in Cincinnati. Worst of all, the financial returns for the year 1827 were meager, with little hope for future improvement.

Wright reiterated her philosophy for Nashoba in an article for the *New Harmony Gazette* and other publications (some editors refused to run it). People who had been shocked by Richardson's revelations had their dismay reinforced by Wright's approval of free love and true racial equality and by her disdain for religion and for competition in industry.

After most of the whites—who had been few in number—left Nashoba, Wright finally admitted defeat. In June 1828 she moved to New Harmony to begin a new phase of her life.

Wright had promised freedom to some 30 slaves still at

Frances Wright
Courtesy of the Library of Congress. Redrawn by Mary Frey,
Lake Superior Press, Marquette, Michigan.

Nashoba, and she honored that pledge. She induced Whitby to return and supervise them, which he did for more than a year. Convinced that in Haiti they would receive good treatment, she in due time chartered a brig to sail them from New Orleans to that island. She delivered them to President Jean Pierre Boyer in February 1830, with his assurance that he would see to their welfare.

One of Wright's biographers, William Waterman, writes: "At best, [Nashoba] was an honest but impracticable attempt to better the condition of mankind." Although Wright retained some property at Nashoba, the venture had cost her more than half of the fortune she had at the time, and it must have shaken her confidence in herself.

At New Harmony, Wright became coeditor of its *Gazette*. Robert Dale Owen had recently taken it over, and Wright anticipated no disagreements with him about editorial policy. A weekly, this publication had been in existence for almost three years. Owen and Wright's stated aim was to present important issues without being hampered by any obligations or allegiances. Eventually they changed the name of the journal to *Free Enquirer*—a title that represented their editorial position.

On Independence Day in 1828, Wright gave a public address to the people of New Harmony despite the Pauline injunction. St. Paul had directed: "Let your women keep silent in the churches; for it is not permitted unto them to speak" (1 Corinthians 15:34). His prohibition was observed in nineteenth-century America, so Wright's role as a lecturer was most unusual. This talk was the first of many she gave over a period of some 20 years in many locales.

The content of Wright's addresses was also radical. She attacked organized religion, then so important in the lives of the people. She was against capital punishment and called for the abolition of imprisonment for debt. Education was one of her favorite topics. At a time when there was no public school system, Wright demanded free education for both sexes and offered her own scheme, which favored boarding schools. She called for legal rights for married women, liberal divorce laws, and birth control. In addition to urging political organization of the working classes to obtain better hours and other reforms, she battled the Second Bank of the United States and the Whigs.

Of course Wright was highly criticized, heckled, and even hated; sometimes it was hard for her to find a place to speak. Often the press simply ignored her. Wright attracted vast crowds, however, especially in the early years of her lecturing career. How did this woman appear to her audience?

According to Robert Dale Owen, she was tall and slender, with curly chestnut hair and blue eyes. A newspaper reported: "[She] is among the tallest of women, being about five feet ten inches high; she walks erect, and is remarkably handsome. Her brow is broad and magnificent; her eyes are large; her face is masculine, but well formed."

Although Wright enjoyed liberal friends in New Harmony, in a few months she moved to New York City. She had already bought the *Gazette,* and her coeditor, Robert Dale Owen, soon moved there too. William Phiquepel D'Arusmont, a New Harmony teacher turned printer, came along to produce the weekly. Robert Jennings, an educator from New Harmony, became a sort of agent for Wright's lectures and in addition served as business manager for the paper. The *Gazette/Free Enquirer* and the lectures were intertwined, one expressing or amplifying the views expressed in the other.

Wright converted a former Baptist church into a Hall of Science consecrated to "the sectarian faith." It was an educational and social center for freethinkers. Here, at a low rental, speakers could express liberal viewpoints to as many as 1200 people. Instruction in various disciplines was available for both adults and children. There was a library and even a dispensary where medical advice was free. A bookstore sold inexpensive works published under the imprint of Wright and Owen.

Camilla, who was in failing health and eventually died in 1829, joined the group with her young baby. She remained married to Whitby for the short time left to her, but she seems to have preferred to live with her sister rather than her husband.

When Fanny Wright made her trip to Haiti in February 1830 to settle her freed slaves there, she was accompanied by D'Arusmont, who became her lover. When she returned to New York, she found Camilla in very poor health. They sailed for France in July—Camilla dying and Fanny pregnant. From that time on, Fanny Wright and her name became more and more remote from the American public.

Five months later the first American birth control tract appeared. The author was Robert Dale Owen, and it was brought out by Wright and Owen, Publishers. Owen wrote this tract as a result of his exposure to the work of a British journalist and freethinker named Richard Carlisle (1790–1843). Carlisle had provided contraceptive information in a pamphlet entitled *Every Woman's Book or, What Is Love?* Robert Dale Owen explained later that in 1828 he had been requested to reprint this pamphlet in the *New Harmony Gazette*. He had refused because he doubted its physiological correctness, considered the style and tone in poor taste, and feared the information would fall into the wrong hands. At the same time, he saluted Carlisle's courage in approaching such a controversial subject. The publication was mentioned in the *Gazette*, but it is not clear who was behind the insertion. At a later date, Owen's enemies demanded that he endorse or repudiate Carlisle's work. Owen was unwilling to give it his unqualified approval; instead he wrote *Moral Physiology; or, A Brief and Plain Treatise on the Population Question*.

The 72-page tract was issued on December 1, 1830, at the price of 37 cents. The frontispiece was a copy of a painting representing a poor mother abandoning her infant at the gate of the Paris Foundling Hospital. She is exclaiming, "Alas! that it should ever have been born!"

Owen's tract was long on socioeconomic issues and short on contraceptive methodology. But the former were very important if prevailing attitudes were to be changed. Several passages (from the tenth edition) are of particular interest:

> If man, then, can obtain control over the most important of instincts, it is, *in principle*, right that he should know it. If men, after obtaining such knowledge, think fit not to use it; if they deem it nobler and more virtuous, to follow each animal impulse, like the beasts in the field and the fowls of the air, without a thought of its consequences, or an enquiry into its nature—then let them do so. The knowledge that they have the power to act more like rational beings, will not injure, if it fail to benefit them. They are at perfect liberty to set it aside, to neglect it, to forget it, if they can. Only let them show common sense enough to permit that others . . . should obtain the requisite knowledge, and follow out their prudent resolutions.

> What would be the possible effect, in social life, if mankind obtained and exercised a control over the instinct of reproduction?

> My settled conviction is—and I am prepared to defend it—that the effect would be salutary, moral, civilizing; that it would prevent many crimes and more unhappiness; that it would lessen intemperance and profligacy; that it would polish the manners and improve the moral feelings; that it would relieve the burdens of the

poor, and the cares of the rich; that it would most essentially benefit the rising generation, by enabling parents generally more carefully to educate, and more comfortably to provide for, their offspring.

No man ought even to *desire* that a woman should become the mother of his children unless it was her express wish, and unless he knew it to be for her welfare, that she should. Her feelings, her interests, should be for him in this matter *an imperative law.* She it is who bears the burden, and therefore with her also should the decision rest. Surely it may well be a question whether ... the whole life of an intellectual, cultivated woman, should be spent in rearing a family of twelve or fifteen children; to the ruin, perhaps, of her constitution, if not to the overstocking of the world. No man ought to require or expect it.

The choice of contraceptive methods was limited in 1830. Owen suggested

complete withdrawal, on the part of the man, immediately previous to emission. *This is, in all cases, effectual.* ... It may be objected, that the practice requires a mental effort and a partial sacrifice. I reply, that, in France, where men consider this, (as it ought ever to be considered, when the interests of the other sex require it) a *point of honour*—all young men must learn to make the necessary effort; and custom renders it easy and a matter of course. As for the sacrifice, shall a trifling (and it is but a very trifling) diminution of physical enjoyment be suffered to outweigh the most important consideration connected with the permanent welfare of those who are the nearest and dearest to us?

Sponges and condoms were also mentioned as contraceptives. The latter was characterized as expensive and the former was known to fail sometimes.

Although Wright was in France when *Moral Physiology* came out, her approval of the project is implied by the fact that she was copublisher. She also publicly voiced approbation of her associate's work by mentioning it in the *Free Enquirer.*

Moral Physiology went through many editions—some issued by publishers other than Wright and Owen—and was generally well received. Richard Leopold, one of Owen's biographers, notes that Wright was the better speaker and Owen the better writer. If this is so, it is fortunate that it was Owen's destiny, not Wright's, to write on an important issue that was bound to offend the prudery then part of the makeup of so many individuals.

The year after *Moral Physiology* was published, a more medically oriented work on birth control appeared—*Fruits of Philosophy*. The author, Charles Knowlton, acknowledged his debt to Owen, and before Wright's Hall of Science was sold in 1831, Knowlton spoke there. The importance of *Fruits* will become apparent in the next chapter.

Soon after the Wright sisters reached Paris, Camilla died. According to Wright biographer Celia Morris Eckhardt, a girl was born to Wright around the beginning of January 1831. She was named Frances Sylva D'Arusmont. Six months later, Wright and D'Arusmont were married, with La Fayette as a witness. On April 14, 1832, a second daughter was born, who survived for only three months. The birthdate of that child was used for Sylva, and mother and daughter maintained the deception.

In the years ahead, Wright would cross the Atlantic several times, resurrect her speaking career, and write again, but her contributions were far less popular than they had been earlier. Why this was so is not known.

Wright's private life appears to have been anything but happy. She became estranged from her husband, and they were involved in a bitter lawsuit concerning her holdings. A divorce was granted in 1850. To add to her mother's sorrow, Sylva lived with her father after her parents' separation and seems to have been devoted to him. Wright died at age 57 from a broken hip and was buried in Cincinnati.

Frances Wright played a small but significant part in the long struggle to obtain reproductive rights. In addition to supporting liberal divorce laws, she argued that birth control would contribute to equality of the sexes. She expressed this idea publicly at a time when most women refused to mention the subject. Her utterances on various matters speak for themselves:

> [American law allows crimes] against the unhappy female who swears away at one and the same moment her person and her property, and, as it but too often is, her peace, her honor, and her life.

> Until some measures shall be adopted for the judicious and equal instruction and protection of every son and daughter born to the Republic, ye cannot be (as I conceive) Republicans. Until exclusive

colleges, paltry common schools, ignorant Sunday schools, and sectarian churches, be replaced by state institutions, founded by a general tax, and supported by the same . . . and, until in these national institutions, the child of your Governor shall be raised with the child of your farmer, and the child of your President with that of your mechanic, ye cannot be . . . Republicans.

I am no Christian, in the sense usually attached to the word. I am neither Jew nor Gentile, Mahomedan [*sic*] nor Theist; I am but a member of the human family, and would accept of truth by whomsoever offered.

The hardest labour is often without a reward adequate to the sustenance of the labourour, . . . whose patient, sedulous industry supplies the community with all its comforts, and the rich with all their luxuries—when he, I say, is brought to an untimely grave by those exertions, which, while sustaining the life of others, cut short his own.

Let us inquire . . . if parents can supply to the creatures they have brought into being, all things requisite to make existence a blessing.

Believe no conviction but your own.

Speak of *change*, and the world is in alarm.

I shall venture the assertion, that, until women assume the place in society which good sense and good feeling alike assign to them, human improvement must advance but feebly.

Biographer Waterman pays Wright this tribute: "A pioneer, she was scoffed at, hooted and reviled, but she showed what the feminine mind was capable of, and having blazed the way, other courageous women were not wanting to follow in her footsteps."

Chapter 2

Annie Besant

We think it more moral to prevent the conception of children, than, after they are born, to murder them by want of food, air and clothing. We advocate scientific checks to population.
— Charles Bradlaugh and Annie Besant, 1877

The First Five Lives of Annie Besant and *The Last Four Lives of Annie Besant* are apt titles for her biography. Birth control was one of her many interests, one that she pursued for a relatively short time and then rejected under the influence of a religious leader who appeared to mesmerize her. Nevertheless, Annie Wood Besant, an Englishwoman, remains an important figure among women advocates of reproductive rights.

The middle child between two brothers, Besant was born in London on October 1, 1847, to Emily (Morris) and William Wood. Her father died five years later and the family moved to Harrow, where Mrs. Wood boarded boys from the famous school. This was officially Besant's home, but in reality she spent little time there.

For the next seven years, a rich woman named Ellen Marryat supervised Besant's education, which included residence in Europe. Marryat's system was progressive except that Calvinism was emphasized. The result was that by 1863 Besant had become a bluestocking. She was a good pianist, and for a Victorian, she showed unusual interest in athletics—in cricket, for instance, and later in horseback riding. Annie Besant was petite and has been described as a beauty.

Early in 1866, Annie met the Reverend Frank Besant, who

taught mathematics at a school for boys. They were married in December 1867, when Annie Besant was just past 20. Besant's interest in religion may have drawn her to her clergyman husband. She had made a study of theology by herself and had yearned to be a martyr. At any rate, she appears to have had an idealized perception of the clergy.

Besant seems to have had little interest in household minutia, and her new life could be described as quiet. This gave her time to write, and although she did not always achieve publication, she began a career that in time produced numerous books, pamphlets, and articles. She also noted, "My dreamy life, . . . kept innocent on all questions of sex, was no preparation for married existence, and left me defenceless to face a rude awakening." This, of course, was not a unique complaint in her era.

A son, Arthur Digby, was born in January 1869, and Mabel Emily arrived in August 1870. Frank Besant was not in favor of family limitation, for which his wife pleaded. Annie Besant's emotional stability is difficult to judge, but it is clear that the marriage was not a happy one.

As Besant's misery deepened, she turned to religion for solace. Gradually she ceased to believe what the church taught, and she finally refused to take communion. She also wrote pamphlets in which she expressed her doubts. In this work she was influenced by a clergyman named Charles Voysey and a radical publisher named Thomas Scott. This caused additional friction with her husband, who was an abusive man. (She maintained he threatened to shoot her.) When he offered her an ultimatum to take communion or leave him, she took the latter course in 1873.

The separation was arranged so that Digby remained with his father, while Mabel lived with her mother. Besant was to receive one quarter of her husband's stipend, and the household effects would remain with him.

Besant tried for a short time to earn her living doing fancy needlework and serving as a governess. She also continued to write pamphlets about religion. In August 1874 she met Charles Bradlaugh, the British social reformer and secularist. Bradlaugh was an advocate of suffrage for women, birth control, free speech, national education, and trade unionism. Besant's relationship with Bradlaugh continued until 1885 and had an important impact on the birth control movement.

An overview of the development of the birth control movement is useful in understanding the roles played by various individuals. It is important to note that highly effective methods of birth control were not used by significant numbers of people until the twentieth century. From time immemorial, some practical means had been known, but by relatively few people because vast communication barriers precluded the wide dissemination of such knowledge. Then too, attitudes had to change before even these methods would be accepted.

Two Egyptian papyri written more than a thousand years before the birth of Christ described ways to prevent pregnancy. One method from 1850 B.C. advised the use of a gummy substance to cover the cervix; another suggested crocodile dung mixed with another substance to form a kind of pessary. Three hundred years later, another papyrus recommended a lint tampon soaked in a mixture of honey and acacia shrub. These papyri gave other methods—for example, the fumigation of the vagina before and after intercourse with smoke from burning dung. Some of the methods probably worked (if they could be tolerated), and their underlying principles would later be developed to produce successful contraception.

The human menstrual cycle was not understood until this century. Although it had been known since 1677 that the semen contained spermatozoa, how a new individual was produced was a matter of speculation until the role of the ovum was appreciated. Such lack of essential knowledge deterred experimentation based on scientific principles and led to erroneous contraceptive advice.

The Egyptians did know that prolonged lactation could prevent pregnancy, and the women constantly nursed their children for as long as three years. Ancient Egypt was also familiar with both male and female castration. John Riddle's 1992 book emphasizes that the ancients used some chemical means of birth control.

The Biblical story of Onan found in the King James version of Genesis 38:7–10 is difficult to interpret:

> And Er, Judah's firstborn, was wicked in the sight of the Lord; and
> the Lord slew him.
> And Judah said unto Onan, Go in unto thy brother's wife, and
> marry her, and raise up seed to thy brother.
> And Onan knew that the seed should not be his; and it came to
> pass, when he went in unto his brother's wife, that he spilled it on
> the ground, lest he should give seed to his brother.
> And the thing which he did displeased the Lord: wherefore he
> slew him also.

A modern dictionary defines *onanism* as (1) coitus interruptus, (2) self-gratification. Regardless of the details of the interpretation, the passage shows clearly that Onan was practicing birth control.

During the second century A.D., Soranus of Ephesus, a Greek physician who worked in Rome, made the important distinction between contraceptives and abortifacients.

Obviously, many of the birth control methods suggested had no hope of success. Among these is one suggested by Pliny the Elder, who held that wearing an amulet of worms taken from a hairy spider would prevent pregnancy.

Rhazes, an Islamic writer who died about A.D. 923, described withdrawal as well as pessaries. The latter were composed of various substances, among them cabbage, pitch, and elephant dung. Islam permitted early abortion, and to achieve this, Rhazes recommended the insertion into the uterus of a probe of wood or tightly wound-up paper.

St. Augustine (A.D. 354–439) was another writer who differentiated birth control from abortion; he condemned both. His was the first clear statement that contraception is a sin, a view reaffirmed by the Roman Catholic hierarchy today.

The origin of the condom is not clear, although a linen sheath was used in the Middle Ages to prevent syphilis. Late in the sixteenth century, this practice improved to the point that the linen was first soaked in a chemical solution and then dried.

There is evidence that condoms were being used by 1666, the time of London's Great Fire. Casanova (1725–98), the adventurer from Venice, used the condom as a contraceptive and not primarily to prevent venereal disease. By his day, animal membranes were in use. After vulcanization was developed around the middle of the last century, the use of rubber condoms increased.

The vaginal sponge seems to have originated in France in the seventeenth century. It became known in Britain much later.

In 1798 the Reverend Thomas Malthus, an Englishman, wrote his *Essay on the Principles of Population*. This work postulated that population will always tend to outrun the food supply. Malthus noted that war, famine, and disease hold population in check. In a revised version (1803), he proposed sexual abstinence and late marriage as checks.

Jeremy Bentham, one of the men whom Fanny Wright impressed, had studied the British poor laws. He quickly realized how overpopulation added to the burden of the poor. Supposedly through a Methodist clergyman named Joseph Townsend, Bentham learned about the vaginal sponge popular in France. Townsend was the author of *A Dissertation on the Poor Laws*. Historians believe that Bentham influenced two men in particular to distribute this information to the poor without associating his name with the sponge.

One of these was Francis Place, born in a private debtor's prison run by his father. Self-educated, he became a successful tailor. His particular interest was radical politics on behalf of the lower classes, and he soon realized the value of birth control for the poor. He had hopes that smaller families would lessen the necessity of child labor and that contraception would make possible earlier marriage. Place envisioned that this in turn would mean fewer illicit affairs and a decreased incidence of venereal disease. In 1823, after consultation with some physicians, he publicized his ideas in some newspapers and also in leaflets that came to be known as the Diabolical Handbills. The vaginal sponge he promoted could be made of "lint, fine wool, cotton, flax or whatever may be at hand." He did not advise the condom, but in some issues of his work, he mentioned withdrawal. Place recruited 17-year-old John Stuart Mill to distribute the Diabolical Handbills to the poor. Mill's work in the population problem was influenced by his seeing the body of a strangled baby in a London park. Mill ultimately became a champion of women's rights and in 1869 was the author of *The Subjection of Women*. Another thinker who was influenced by Bentham was Richard Carlisle, author of *Every Woman's Book*, previously mentioned.

Thus by the 1870s the British public had at least some exposure to the idea of birth control. The medical profession did not back the idea, however. Regarding the "vile practice" of birth control, one physician wrote in 1879: "Suffice it to say that Onan's crime is imitated; coverings used by the males, plugs and injections by the females." Referring to placement in the uterus of devices originally intended for pathological conditions but used to prevent conception, he noted "to what degree of degradation some [doctors] have fallen."

Charles Bradlaugh (1833–91), the son of a poor legal clerk, also became active in the birth control movement. After serving briefly in the British army, he too became a legal clerk and then in 1860 became editor of the *National Reformer*, a magazine that advocated freethinking. Bradlaugh was an atheist and also a neo–Malthusian. The latter term refers to one who accepts Malthus's views on population but also advocates birth control within marriage rather than late marriage as a check on overpopulation. Bradlaugh lost no time in hiring Besant at one guinea a week to write for his magazine. She also joined the National Secular Society, in which he was prominent.

While Besant was still living with her husband in a village named Sibsey, she once went to his church to practice on the organ. Alone there, she used the occasion to deliver a lecture. "I shall never forget the feeling of power and delight—but especially of power—that came upon me as I sent my voice ringing down the aisles. ... if ever the chance came to me of public work, this power of melodious utterance should at least win hearing of any message I had to bring," she wrote in her autobiography. After her separation from her husband, she developed into a first-class lecturer, using her talent to promote freethinking and whatever issue struck her fancy. According to George Bernard Shaw, she was "the greatest orator in England, and possibly in Europe."

As a freethinker, Besant became a member of the Malthusian League. This had been founded in the 1860s by Dr. George Drysdale (1824–1904), and other Drysdales would be associated with it. (Holland's Dr. Aletta Jacobs met Dr. Drysdale and Besant in London when she was just beginning her career as a doctor.)

It was Besant's interest in birth control that led to the reissue of Knowlton's *Fruits of Philosophy*, which had first appeared in England in 1834. It not only justified birth control but made the following statement: "it is the duty for him who has a knowledge of [contraception] to convey it to those who have it not; for, by so doing, he furthers the cause of human happiness." Knowlton's work was unusual in that it recommended vaginal douching. He was confident that water was an effective agent but suggested that adding alum and a variety of vegetable substances then used in medicine could be useful. He also mentioned vinegar. The book caused its author brief imprisonment, but he estimated that by 1881 more than a quarter of a million copies had been sold.

In 1876 a British bookseller named Henry Cook added illustrations to *Fruits*. Cook was sentenced to two years at hard labor under the 1857 obscene publication act. Charles Watt, a freethought publisher associated with Besant and Bradlaugh, had put out an edition of *Fruits*, and he too was prosecuted. Pleading "guilty in law," he got off relatively easily. The terms demanded that he cease publication and destroy his supply of copies.

Such repressive action rankled the freethinking liberals Bradlaugh and Besant. Highly sensitive to the differences in the British world between the "haves" and the "have nots," they saw the misery caused by crowding, malnutrition, poor housing, and lack of opportunity and realized that knowing how to limit family size could do much to improve the lot of the poor. So they planned to test what they termed the right of publication.

In 1877 Bradlaugh and Besant reissued Knowlton's book, using the prosecuted edition but correcting errors in printing and grammar. Before *Fruits* went on sale, they delivered copies to the chief clerk of the London magistrates, to the police, and to the solicitor for the city of London. They were arrested and released on their own recognizances. Their indictment was for vitiating and corrupting morals and inciting people to "indecent, obscene, unnatural and immoral practices."

At the trial that followed, the prosecutor declared: "I say that this is a dirty, filthy book, and the test of it is that no human being would allow that book on his table, no decently educated English husband would allow even his wife to have it." The jury condemned

Annie Besant
Courtesy of the National Picture Gallery, London.

the book but exonerated the defendants from a corrupt motive. Lord Chief Justice Cockburn said he would have to interpret their verdict to mean guilty.

At the sentencing, the defendants refused to stop selling the book. They were each given a six-month prison term and fined. Bradlaugh, who had an excellent knowledge of law, applied for a writ of error. A few months later the Cockburn decision was reversed, due to a technicality. This action freed Besant and Bradlaugh, who at that point had served no time.

While the appeal had been pending, Frank Besant had applied to the Chancery Division of the High Court of Justice to obtain custody of Mabel. He charged Annie with propagating atheism, and also alleged that with "an Infidel Lecturer and Author named Bradlaugh," she had published "an indecent and obscene pamphlet." The clergyman won his case, but Besant was allowed some contact with her daughter. (When the children came of age, they both chose to be with their mother, and their father severed contact with them.)

Besant's *The Law of Population: Its Bearing Upon Human Conduct and Morals* came out in 1877 at a cost of six cents. Written because *Fruits* was out of date, it discussed coitus interruptus, douching , the vaginal sponge, and in later editions, the rubber cervical cap. Unfortunately, Besant gave incorrect information on the "safe period" of the menstrual cycle. She condemned abortion as a method of birth control: "When conception has taken place, then prevention is no longer permissible, and a new life having been made, the destruction of that life would be criminal. . . . Surely the prevention of conception is far better than the procuring of abortion." To her credit, Besant entered a plea to the medical profession for research aimed at effective and acceptable contraceptives. By 1891 some 175,000 copies of her book had been sold in various countries without court action in Britain. It must have pleased her that the readership was principally working people.

In 1878, in response to the Bradlaugh-Besant prosecution, another Drysdale, Dr. Charles R., brother of George, spearheaded the formation of a medical branch of the Malthusian League. He was joined in this endeavor by his wife, Dr. Alice Vickery, one of the first women physicians in England.

Four years later, the Dutch Malthusian League started medical service under Dr. Aletta Jacobs. The target group consisted of poor women and their infants, and the clinic offered contraceptive advice. This information was improved after Dr. Jacobs learned about the vaginal spring diaphragm. (See page 56.)

After the trial, Besant became more interested in issues other than population control. Her friendship with Bradlaugh continued until 1885. From letters, they appear to have been in love. He was married, however, although he was estranged from his alcoholic wife (who died in 1877), and Annie was legally married to Frank Besant.

Wishing to increase her knowledge, Besant took classes at the South Kensington branch of London University, which had begun to admit women for degrees. One examiner told her beforehand that even if she did well, he would fail her; he did not approve of her atheism and other activities that seemed immoral to him. During this period of her life, her companion was her former instructor, Edward Aveling, who interested her in science.

In 1885 Besant met and became friendly with George Bernard Shaw. His influence was sufficient to cause her to join the Fabian Society. The Fabians were opposed to the revolutionary theory of Marx and contended instead that socialism would evolve with proper indoctrination of targeted groups.

Socialism eventually replaced free thought as Besant's consuming interest. A Socialist named Herbert Burrows played a large part in this. It is interesting to note, however, that Bradlaugh was very opposed to socialism.

While Besant still resided in England, her interest in education manifested itself in her election to the London school board.

In 1889 socialism's appeal gave way to theosophy, to which Besant was converted by the Russian-born Helena Petrovna Hahn Blavatsky. Theosophy is a philosophic system having affinities with mysticism. Madame Blavatsky promoted Hindu-oriented doctrines.

"I gave up Neo-Malthusianism in April 1891, its renunciation being part of the outcome of two years' instruction from Mdme. H. P. Blavatsky," Besant stated in her autobiography. She even refused to reprint the "Law of Population" or to sell the copyright.

After Besant moved to India in 1893, she put her energy into politics and education. In 1898 she founded the Central Hindu College at Benares, now Varansi. (This was merged with the Hindu University of Benares in 1921.) Some years later, she established the Indian Home Rule League. By 1917 she was president of the Indian National Congress. Later, however, she disagreed with Mahatma Gandhi, the great Indian political and spiritual leader.

During her eighth "life," Besant was under the influence of the Brahmin occultist, Professor Gyanendra Chakravarti. In 1925 Besant proclaimed her protégé, Jiddu Krishnamurti, the Messiah and promoted his cult. The following year, she traveled with him to England and the United States.

The year 1924 marked the fiftieth anniversary of Besant's entry into public life. She was given a party at Queen's Hall, and various dignitaries unable to attend honored her by sending congratulatory messages.

Annie Besant died in India in 1933.

Besant's great concern was always to improve the lot of working people. From the podium and in her writing, she pressed for smaller families, better education, more freedom, world peace, and shorter working hours. Philip Snowdon (1864–1937), the British statesman who knew poverty from personal experience, paid her this tribute: "no woman of this generation has devoted supreme gifts of oratory and intellect to great humanitarian causes with such energy and disinterestness as Mrs. Besant."

Chapter 3

Emma Goldman

We have done a great deal toward popularizing the question of [birth control], and as far as I know, E.G. was the first and last to give actual methods from the platform.
—*Mother Earth*, 1916

In Iowa City, Iowa, the Emma Goldman Clinic for Women has existed since 1973. It offers pregnancy-related services, contraceptive services, and preventive health care. A flyer explains that Emma Goldman was an educator and public advocate for birth control at a time when such action was prohibited by laws. Although birth control was not Goldman's primary focus, her activities in the field were important enough to influence Margaret Sanger, who would become the foremost leader of the movement in the United States.

Goldman was born on June 27, 1869, in what was then the Russian province of Kovna (now in Lithuania). Her parents were Abraham and Taube (Bienowich) Goldman, both Jews. Taube's first husband had died, leaving two daughters named Lena and Helena. Three sons were born after Emma.

Goldman's childhood was not happy, chiefly due to her father's harsh treatment of his children. Abraham appears to have been a frustrated man, keenly aware of the lack of opportunity for Jews in Russia. He was also disappointed that Emma was not a boy. A violent man, he intimidated his children by beating them. To add to their uneasiness, there was constant quarreling between him and his wife. To Emma, her mother seemed cold.

31

Helena, her older half-sister, provided the affection not offered by her mother.

When Goldman was six, the family moved to Papile, where her father ran an inn and also managed the government stage-coach service. But after an accident, he lost that job.

The next move was to Königsberg (Kaliningrad), which was then the capital of Prussia. Here Goldman attended school, passing the entrance examinations to a German gymnasium, but the religion teacher refused her a certificate of good character on the grounds that she did not have the proper respect for authority. Without that certificate, she could not be admitted to the gymnasium.

Abraham Goldman had taken charge of a cousin's dry goods store in St. Petersburg, where the family joined him. Emma loved the culture and excitement of that great city. Unfortunately, after a few months, she had to leave school to find work. She did piece work at home, knitting shawls; later she worked in a glove factory and then in a corset factory.

It was in St. Petersburg that Emma Goldman learned that women played important roles in the revolutionary movement. She was also influenced by Nikolai Chernishevsky's *What Is to Be Done?* The heroine of this work leads an independent life and is able to contribute to society; this appealed to Goldman.

At 15, Goldman refused to be part of a customary arranged marriage, hoping instead for more education. Her autobiography recounts her father's reply: "Girls do not have to learn much! All a Jewish daughter needs to know is how to prepare gefulltefish, cut fine noodles and give the man plenty of children."

Following the lead of her sister Lena, Helena decided to emigrate to the United States. She offered to pay Emma's fare. Abraham Goldman was determined to keep Emma, then 16, in Russia, but he relented when she threatened to jump into the Neva River. In December, 1885, the sisters departed St. Petersburg; from Hamburg they took the *Elbe* to New York.

Emma and Helena's destination was Rochester, New York, the home of Lena and her husband. His job as a tinsmith brought in only $12 a week, so two more mouths to feed put a strain on the family resources. The young women quickly realized that the streets of America were not paved with gold. Helena found work retouching negatives, and Emma worked 10½ hours a day sewing coats for a salary of $2.50 a week. She was employed by Garson and Meyer, who ran what was considered a model factory.

Emma Goldman soon asked for a raise, but was told by Garson himself to leave if she did not like the conditions. Garson was a German Jew, and Goldman felt that he took advantage of Russian immigrants, whom he termed "hands." Eighteen years later, when she was famous, Goldman had the satisfaction of saying to him, "It isn't the saving of pennies that makes people rich; it is the labor of your 'hands' and their ruthless exploitation that has created your wealth."

Goldman's next job paid $4 per week and the owner was less repressive. In his factory she met Jacob Kersner, also a Jewish immigrant from Russia.

In 1886 the rest of the Goldmans moved to Rochester from St. Petersburg, where the treatment of Jews had become intolerable. Helena and Emma moved in with their family.

Kersner's attentions to a lonely Emma Goldman were much appreciated. And the fact that he had graduated from the Odessa Gymnasium impressed her. After a four-month courtship, they became engaged. In 1887, when Goldman was not yet 18, they were married by a rabbi.

The marriage was not a success. Kersner was impotent; and he lost much of his $15 a week salary at cards. As a married woman, Goldman had left her job, so making ends meet was a constant difficulty. In a short time, they obtained a divorce.

Goldman then worked briefly in New Haven. When she returned to Rochester, Kersner again sought her out. His threat of suicide moved her to remarry him, but things went no better the second time and she left him permanently. Because the Jewish community did not support divorce, censure of her action was severe.

Goldman moved to New York City in 1889, when she was 20 and ready to change the world. Her interest in anarchy had evolved steadily. It had begun in Russia, where young radicals were resisting injustice and oppression. Already disappointed that conditions in the United States seemed little better, Goldman had become bitterly disillusioned with democracy because of the hanging of the anarchists convicted in the 1886 Haymarket Square riot.

In the 1880s, labor was seeking reforms, especially an eight-hour day, and Chicago workers were leaders in this effort. On May 4, 1886, a striker was accidentally killed in a gathering at the McCormick Harvesting Machine Company. The next day, anarchists called a protest meeting at Haymarket Square. An unknown person threw a bomb into the crowd that killed seven policemen; scores of persons were injured in the panic that followed. August Spies and seven other anarchist labor leaders were convicted of inciting violence; they had supposedly conspired with the unknown murderer, although no connection was demonstrated. Spies and three others were hanged on November 11, 1887. Another leader committed suicide. Six years later the governor of Illinois pardoned the three serving prison terms.

Goldman was familiar with the story, and *Die Freiheit*, a German paper edited by Johann Most, had increased her interest in anarchism. She began to read *Die Freiheit* regularly and to absorb everything she could find out about anarchy.

Goldman had brought a sewing machine to New York. She had taken a course in dressmaking (without her husband's knowledge) and hoped to earn her living at home rather than in a shop because she hated shop restrictions and also yearned for time to read and further her education.

Soon Goldman was settled in a room that cost $3 a month and had found work she could do there—sewing on silk waists and sometimes making dresses. "The work was exhausting, but it freed me from the factory and its galling discipline," she declared.

Almost immediately Goldman met Johann Most, the anarchist editor of *Die Freiheit*, who noted her enthusiasm for his cause and encouraged her development as a lecturer. The association with Most deepened her understanding of anarchism.

The word anarchism comes from the Greek and means no government. According to the theory of anarchism, the state should be abolished and replaced by free agreements between individuals as a means of bringing equality and justice. The theory holds that men are basically good but are corrupted by artificial institutions such as the state or centralized authority that impede individual development. In time Goldman would speak out against government, capitalism, and militarism. She had an antipathy to religion and did not approve of legal organizations and voting. Opposed to both legal marriage and religious marriage, she supported free love, defending birth control and also homosexuality. At first she believed in violence as a means of obtaining a just end, but this view moderated as she grew older.

It was Alexander Berkman who introduced Goldman to Most. A member of a privileged family, Berkman had also immigrated from Russia, arriving in 1888. Almost immediately he had become involved in anarchist activity in New York City. Although he had a gymnasium education, he had worked at menial jobs in the United States.

In a short time, Berkman, known as Sasha, and Goldman were involved sexually. Their relationship, in one form or another, would last until Berkman's death. With a young woman and a young man named Fedya, who was Berkman's first cousin, they moved into an apartment where they practiced communal living. As advocates of free love, Goldman and Fedya saw nothing unusual in their becoming lovers.

Despite her dedication to anarchism, which involved doing as much as possible towards the betterment of common people, Goldman believed in spending money for "beautiful things," which included flowers and music. In fact, she looked on beauty as a necessity rather than a luxury. Berkman, on the other hand, believed that it was inconsistent for an anarchist to enjoy luxuries while the people lived in poverty.

By 1892 Fedya, Sasha, and Emma had tried to earn a living in various ways, none of them particularly successful. The Homestead Strike brought about a great change in their lives.

Andrew Carnegie's steel plant in Homestead, Pennsylvania, was struck by the workers. Henry Clay Frick, its manager, was determined to crush the unions and brought in strikebreakers and more than 300 private Pinkerton guards to protect them. Fighting broke out between the two sides, with deaths and injuries resulting. Berkman announced his plan to murder Frick and was backed up by Goldman, who then believed that "the end justified all means." There was not enough money for her to go to Pennsylvania with her lover, but she borrowed money for him to buy a revolver. He shot Frick but did not kill him. Berkman was sentenced to 22 years in prison; Goldman's role in the affair was not recognized.

Goldman worked with others to obtain a commutation of Berkman's sentence, and she was his faithful correspondent. (He was released from prison after 14 years.) Berkman's fate also deepened her already strong commitment to anarchism.

Meanwhile, there were other men in Goldman's life. One of them was Edward Brady. He introduced her to the great classics of English and French literature, and through him she met radical writers and intellectuals. A gentle man ten years her senior, he wanted children, but she had decided against motherhood, chiefly so she could devote all her energy to her "cause." (Apparently she would remain sterile unless she had an operation, which she declined.) Goldman knew that Brady resented the life she led that kept them apart so much of the time. Although she loved him, she felt he wanted "to rob me of all that is more precious to me than life." Their involvement ended in 1897.

As Goldman delivered her views on anarchism in various parts of the country, she attracted large audiences and at the same time caused concern to those in authority. During the depression of 1893, she addressed the unemployed thus: "Demonstrate before the palaces of the rich; demand work. If they do not give you work, demand bread. If they deny you both, take bread. It is your sacred right!"

Goldman's statements brought a charge of "inciting to riot," and she was required to stand trial. Found guilty, she was sentenced to a year at Blackwell's Island Penitentiary. A woman newspaper reporter who had interviewed Goldman before the trial described her as an attractive young woman of about five feet, weighing 120 pounds, with turned-up nose, blue-gray eyes and light brown hair; she wore shell-rimmed glasses.

The prison term had compensations. It gave Goldman the opportunity to read many books written in English. Both she and Berkman were more fluent in German than English, which was beneficial, since most of their activity was directed to immigrants. Nevertheless, Goldman desired to perfect her English. Following an illness, she was assigned to work at the prison hospital, where she spent seven months. During that time, she learned skills that later enabled her to earn money as a practical nurse. After a term of ten months, Goldman was released—to become a sort of martyr of anarchism.

Practical nursing was not lucrative; more formal training commanded better wages. In 1895 Fedya, now a newspaper artist, paid for Goldman to study for a year in Vienna at the Allgemeines Krankenhaus. She managed to fit in a lecture tour in England and Scotland en route. Vienna offered her undreamed of experiences such as hearing a Sigmund Freud lecture, seeing Eleonora Duse act and hearing the entire *Ring des Nibelungen*.

Back again in the United States, Goldman found work as a midwife for the poor and later described the situation of the women she served:

> Their squalid surroundings, the dull and inert submission to their lot, made me realize the colossal work yet to be done to bring about the change our movement was struggling to achieve.
>
> Still more impressed was I by the fierce, blind struggle of the women of the poor against frequent pregnancies. Most of them lived in continual dread of conception; the great mass of married women submitted helplessly, and when they found themselves pregnant, their alarm and worry would result in the determination to get rid of their unexpected offspring. It was incredible what fantastic methods despair could invent.... Having a large brood of children, often many more than the weekly wage of the father could provide for, each additional child was a curse, "a curse of God," as orthodox Jewish women and Irish Catholics repeatedly told me.

Goldman did not do abortions when she was requested to because she did not feel competent to do so. "It was not any moral consideration for the sanctity of life; a life unwanted and forced into abject poverty did not seem sacred to me," she wrote later. Goldman had another reason not to risk imprisonment: "my interests embraced the entire social problem, not merely a single aspect of it, and I would not jeopardize my freedom for one part of the human struggle. I refused to perform abortions and I knew no methods to prevent conception."

When Goldman asked three physicians for advice on the matter of birth control, she received none. In 1909, however, an opportunity came for her to attend a secret meeting of the Neo-Malthusian Congress in Paris. There she met the Drysdales and others who instructed her.

The generosity of two affluent men made Goldman's presence in Europe possible; they guaranteed her expenses for five years while she studied medicine in Switzerland.* On the way there, she had found in London a new lover, an immigrant revolutionist. When her benefactors decided that the medical course seemed secondary to Goldman's political activity and her love life, they withdrew their support.

When Goldman began to lecture again at home, she added birth control to her subjects. She did not discuss methods but gave the information in private if it was requested. Contraception fit very naturally into the concept of individual freedom, which was Goldman's thesis.

By 1901, Goldman was speaking to audiences that included many native-born Americans. (In fact, she was later criticized for spending so much effort on informed Americans rather than on immigrants who needed to be educated.) Her English was now excellent, and press coverage made her known to a vast reading public.

Goldman gained more notoriety when President McKinley was shot. The assassin was 29-year-old Leon Czolgosz, who admitted that he had heard Goldman lecture in Cleveland and had later spoken with her in Chicago. The police tried to make him implicate her, but he was steadfast in her insistence that the idea of shooting the president was his alone. The press produced sensational stories, but ultimately the police had to admit that Goldman was in no way connected with the act.

As she grew older, Goldman turned away from violence, no matter how provocative the situation. In the memory of some, however, she would remain indirectly responsible for the death of William McKinley.

Until the First World War, opportunities for women to study medicine in first-class universities in the United States were limited. American women preferred to enter foreign medical schools, especially those of Switzerland and France.

Always expanding her intellectual horizons, in 1905 Goldman began to add to her lectures titles such as "The Revolutionary Spirit of the Modern Drama." The next year she founded *Mother Earth* "to voice without fear every unpopular cause, and to aim for unity between revolutionary effort and artistic expression." Following Berkman's release in 1907, he became editor of *Mother Earth*. Since Goldman was out-of-town at least half of the time, this was a good move. The two remained close, but they both had changed a great deal in 14 years.

In 1908, when she was 39, Goldman met Ben Reitman, who would be her lover for ten years, although he was some ten years her junior. Born to immigrant Jews, Reitman knew mostly outcasts and down-and-outs. A runaway at 11, his travels had brought him into contact with other hobos. While he held a menial job at the Chicago Polyclinic, he impressed his superiors so much that he was encouraged to become a doctor, which he succeeded in doing. His patients were the same type of people he had known as a youngster, and he became an advocate for the unemployed. His familiarity with prostitutes spurred an interest in venereal disease prevention, and later he would take part in establishing the first venereal disease clinic at the Cook County jail. Although he had Goldman's desire to help the poor, Reitman was not a dedicated anarchist. No atheist either, he had become a Baptist.

In the beginning, Reitman acted as Goldman's manager. Her lectures required extensive planning, especially because it was often difficult to find people willing to rent a hall to "Red Emma." There were always hecklers, the police were generally unreceptive to anarchists, and rentals to less controversial persons were preferable.

The relationship between Goldman and Reitman did not always run smoothly. He engaged in what she termed "compulsive infidelity," and he seems to have regarded her as a mother figure.

In 1915 Reitman distributed, as did Goldman, a pamphlet he had written entitled "How and Why the Poor Should Not Have Many Children." It gave information about condoms, pessaries, and douches. The couples' action was dangerous because it violated the Comstock Law.

Emma Goldman
Courtesy of the Library of Congress.

For almost one hundred years, the influence of one man, Anthony Comstock, remained a significant obstruction to progress in winning women's reproductive rights in the United States. This influence outlived him and even moved George Bernard Shaw to coin the word Comstockery to describe it. Comstock came from humble beginnings, obtaining power from the strength of his convictions. Although he was a zealot with little formal education, biographers Heywood Broun and Margaret Leech make it clear that he had some admirable qualities.

Anthony Comstock was born in 1844 in New Canaan, Connecticut, to Polly (Lockwood) and Thomas Anthony Comstock. Both parents were descended from Puritans, and attendance at services in a Congregational church was part of the family routine. Thomas Comstock owned a prosperous farm. Polly bore ten children, seven of whom survived childhood. Tony, as he was called, adored his mother and absorbed the Bible stories she told him before he could read. She died when he was ten, but he never forgot her. Religion seems to have become a continuing and all-embracing part of his life while he was still a youth.

In December 1863, at the age of 19, Comstock enlisted in the Union Army, Seventeenth Connecticut. An older brother had died as a result of wounds received at Gettysburg, and Comstock regarded himself as a replacement. The diary that he began when he became a soldier provides insight into his character. In an early entry he complained of "the air resounding with the oathes of wicked men." He also recounted that three of the seven recruits with him pledged not to swear, drink, or use tobacco during the three years of their enlistments. When whiskey was allotted, Comstock accepted it and then poured it onto the ground—an act that in all probability did not add to his popularity.

The summer of 1865 saw Comstock mustered out of the army without participation in major combat. The family farm had failed and his father had remarried, so Comstock did a short stint in New Haven as a grocery clerk and bookkeeper.

Attracted to New York, Comstock soon found a job as a porter in a dry goods company. He advanced there, and by 1871 was earning $27 a week selling dry goods for a concern on Broadway.

That year Comstock married Margaret Hamilton, a woman ten years his senior. He bought a small home in Brooklyn, which was an improvement on the boarding houses where he had lived as a bachelor. The marriage seems to have been a happy one. A daughter was born late in 1871 but died before her first birthday. A short time later, Comstock brought home a baby girl just born to a woman who was dying. The child was named Adele and was legally adopted by the Comstocks. She was mentally retarded and difficult, but her adopted father loved her dearly, and she him.

Much of Comstock's adult life was a crusade against obscenity, which included anything having a tendency to suggest impure and libidinous thoughts to the young and inexperienced. This applied particularly to the many single young men from rural America who came to New York to seek work. Comstock once wrote: "[Erotic literature] breeds lust.... It robs the soul of manly virtues and imprints upon the mind of youth, visions that throughout life curse the man or woman.... This traffic has made rakes and libertines in society." His antiobscenity campaign began in earnest in the 1870s and was related to the Young Men's Christian Association (YMCA).

Begun in London in 1884, the YMCA soon became known in the United States by providing for the spiritual and physical needs of male youths. By the time of the Civil War, several branches formed the United States Christian Commission, noted for its work in the military. Following the war, the YMCA in New York urged passage of a state law to regulate saloons and to suppress obscene literature. Such a bill did pass in 1868, but it was not as effective as the YMCA had hoped.

According to carryover from British common law, obscenity was an offense. In 1815 the state of Pennsylvania had ruled it a crime; six years later Vermont had an obscenity law. Massachusetts and Connecticut ruled against obscenity in the 1830s. An 1842 federal law prohibited the importation of indecent pictures and articles, and in 1865 Congress ruled that books and pictures of such a nature could not be mailed. Rules were on the books, but were they enforced?

Comstock thought not. He wrote to an official of the YMCA in New York to ask the help of that organization in his personal battle against obscenity. The letter came to the attention of the president, Morris K. Jessup. Rich and influential, Jessup financed a Comstock venture in buying erotic books and plates so that they would no longer be in circulation as corrupting influences. Within two years, the YMCA had provided Comstock with around $8500 to further this type of activity. These YMCA officials believed, as did Comstock, that erotic materials were "feeders for brothels." At first Comstock was concerned mainly with making arrests and confiscating what was offensive. In his 1880 book, *Frauds Exposed*, he explained, "I found laws inadequate, and public sentiment worse than dead because of an appetite that had been formed for salacious reading."

Comstock soon recognized the loopholes in existing laws and sought to strengthen the position that the mail must not be used to transmit anything that could be considered obscene. Early in 1873, he was in Washington showing members of Congress examples of what had already passed through the Postal Service in violation of the law. His stay in the capital city was supported by the YMCA.

The upshot of Comstock's efforts was the passage in 1873 of a strong bill regarding the mailing of obscene matter within the United States, including the District of Columbia and the territories. For the first time, information on "the prevention of conception" came under the definition of obscene. The "Act for the Suppression of Trade in and Circulation of Obscene Literature and Articles of Immoral Use" also made it a felony to have in one's possession "any article whatever, for the prevention of conception, or for causing unlawful abortion." As a matter of serious consequence, the federal law rapidly influenced many states to enact their own "little Comstock laws." For example, 24 states made laws that prohibited the transportation of contraceptives and abortifacients.

The legislators appointed Comstock himself a special agent for the U.S. Post Office, with the authority to arrest violators. The U.S. Post Office also conferred on its new appointee free transportation on all lines carrying mail.

So, at the age of 29, a new career opened up for Comstock, and he soon severed his connections with the dry goods business. He was eligible for a salary from the U.S. Post Office, but for many years did not accept it because he was supported by the YMCA through its Committee for the Suppression of Vice. There is ample evidence that Comstock was an honest man, not susceptible to bribery. The new agent did his work well. He was successful in organizing several Societies for the Suppression of Vice;

Boston's group was called "The New England Watch and Ward Society." Comstock used ingenuity and energy to obtain necessary evidence and also proved to be a master of trickery. Besides confiscating large amounts of offending material, he made frequent arrests.

One victim, apprehended in 1878, was an Englishwoman named Anna Lohman. She had been a midwife and later provided abortions. Known as Madame Restell, she lived well in a fine residence at 52nd Street and Fifth Avenue. Although she was practicing illegally, she had little interference from the law. According to the *Congregationalist*, "By skillfully playing the part of an applicant for her services, Mr. Comstock not only entrapped the woman, but secured instruments, medicines, etc." Madame Restell offered her nemesis $40,000, but Comstock did not take bribes. Seeing the handwriting on the wall, Restell, then 67, slit her throat. Hers was not the only suicide precipitated by Comstock's zeal; according to his count, she was the fifteenth.

Hounded by the special agent, Ida Craddock killed herself in 1902 by inhaling gas. Her crime was mailing a pamphlet entitled *The Wedding Night*, of which she was the author. Its content would now be classified under sex education. Although it was well received in some quarters, Comstock determined it improper for mailing.

In 1913 Comstock claimed that after 14 years, he had convicted more than 3500 persons and had destroyed 160 tons of obscene literature. He died two years later. Towards the end of his life, his power, in terms of arrests and confiscations, had greatly diminished. Nevertheless, his influence remained until 1971, when the last restrictive state law was removed.

In later life Comstock owned a comfortable home in Summit, New Jersey. Jennie Hamilton, his sister-in-law, lived there as an invalid. From his modest means, he also contributed to the support of his half-siblings. Throughout his life, he had a genuine love of children and wrote in 1873 about protecting "the young of our land from the leprosy of this vile trash."

Comstock's influence affected art to some degree; Shaw incurred his disfavor with regard to *Mrs. Warren's Profession* and the famous "September Morning" came under his purview. Comstock's activity in this area, however, seems to have been relatively innocuous. It is even conceded that his efforts against quacks and vendors of patent medicine were useful. Regardless of Comstock's virtues and good intentions, Comstockery seriously retarded progress in birth control, sex education, and related areas. But we must bear in mind that many Americans of Anthony Comstock's day agreed with him.

In 1914 Margaret Sanger was indicted for publication of *Woman Rebel*. Then early in 1915, William Sanger was arrested for selling *Family Limitation*. "According to Goldman, "[These events] made me aware that the time had come when I must either stop lecturing on the subject or do it practical justice. I felt that I must share with them the consequences of the birth control issue."

On March 15, 1915, Goldman frankly discussed the use of various contraceptives. Her mixed audience included physicians, lawyers, businessmen, and Comstock detectives. To her surprise, there was no arrest.

In August in Portland, Oregon, Goldman and Reitman were charged with "circulating literature of an illegal character." A municipal court found them guilty and fined them, but when the case was appealed to a circuit court, their conviction was set aside because of insufficient evidence.

Although Goldman lectured on birth control in various cities as she worked her way home, she escaped arrest. But on February 11, 1916, in New York City, she was finally arrested for a lecture "on a medical question" at the New Star Casino. Found guilty, she was given the choice of paying a $100 fine or serving 15 days in the workhouse. She chose the latter.

Goldman continued to discuss contraceptive methods from the platform until early in 1917, with only one arrest, which was followed by acquittal. She now felt that she had done enough for that particular cause and was content to leave the issue in the hands of others.

Goldman opposed the entry of the United States into World War I and led opposition against the draft. In 1917 she was sentenced to two years in prison; she was released in 1919.

At that time, there was a considerable degree of hysteria about communism in the United States and prejudice against anarchists was running high. One result was that Goldman and Berkman, along with 247 others, were deported to the Soviet Union. Berkman had never become an American citizen. Goldman had derived citizenship through Kersner, but the government denaturalized him in 1908, in a move that was presumably illegal, and then revoked Goldman's citizenship the following year.

By 1923 Goldman had written a book about her experiences in Russia titled *My Disillusionment in Russia*. She had remained there only briefly, disappointed that the revolution had not brought about the changes she envisioned. In the years ahead, she lived, among other places, in Sweden, Germany, England, and France. Not always welcome, she felt insecure as a woman without a country. In 1925 she married James Colton, who offered her his name solely so that she could become a British subject. During the Spanish Civil War, she worked for the antifascist cause. She died in Toronto in 1940.

The United States Immigration and Naturalization Service allowed Goldman's remains to be returned to Chicago, where she was buried, fittingly, in the Waldheim Cemetery, near the graves of her heroes, the convicted Haymarket Square rioters. One of Goldman's biographers, Richard Drinnon, has paid her this tribute: "To the final breath she waged an unrelenting fight for the free individual."

Chapter 4

Margaret Sanger

I believed it was my duty to place motherhood on a higher
level than enslavement and accident. For these beliefs I
was denounced, [and] arrested....
—Margaret Sanger, 1953

The year was 1912, the place a tenement apartment on New
York's Lower East Side. Sadie Sachs, a woman of 28, had just
died from a self-induced abortion, and her husband was discon-
solate.

The young nurse who had been called to the case had bitter
memories. A few months before, she had helped the same patient
to recover from septicemia, or blood poisoning, the result of an
abortion. With three children already, Sadie had made up her
mind not to have another. She had pleaded with the nurse for
some magic way to escape another pregnancy. The nurse knew of
no way, but approached the doctor for help. His advice to Sadie
was "Tell Jake to sleep on the roof."

The nurse was Margaret Sanger, and Sadie Sachs's death
spurred in her an unrelenting effort that ultimately toppled Comstockery and brought birth control to all who wanted it.

Sanger's parents were Michael Hennessey Higgins and Anne
(Purcell) Higgins, and she was born September 14, 1879 (not
1883, as she sometimes claimed), in Corning, New York. Each
parent appears to have had an important influence on her life.

Michael Higgins had immigrated from Ireland and had served
as a Union drummer boy in the Civil War. Higgins made a

47

precarious living by carving headstones for graves. Priding himself on being a freethinker, he numbered among his heroes Henry George, founder of the single tax movement, and the atheist Robert Ingersoll. The ideas of George and Ingersoll were in conflict with the Roman Catholic Church, and Sanger herself soon became an unyielding foe of Catholicism.

Michael Higgins's wife, Anne, was a devout Catholic. She had tuberculosis, which was probably exacerbated by frequent pregnancies. Of eighteen pregnancies, seven had resulted in miscarriages, but eleven growing children constituted a heavy burden in a family where the father's commissions for carvings were sporadic and uncertain. (Margaret Sanger came to blame her father for so many pregnancies, but had birth control been available to Anne Higgins, there is no certainty that she would have used it.) In such a household, much of the care of the children and the home naturally devolved on the older girls.

Sanger was unhappy in Corning, particularly because the family was poor. She had been baptized and confirmed in the Catholic church, thanks to her mother's insistence, but the child of freethinker Michael Higgins was not warmly received into the fold; Sanger knew that she was an outsider. To escape from Corning, Sanger managed to enroll at Claverack, a coeducational non–Catholic boarding school in the Catskills. Her older sisters, Mary and Nan, helped with the expenses, and Sanger herself was able to pay some of her way by working in the school kitchen. She did not remain at Claverack long enough to graduate, but she enjoyed the experience and it broadened her education.

Anne Higgins died in 1899. Sanger had been ordered home by her father prior to this date, and as the sixth child and third daughter, she was needed by the family after her mother's death. Her older sisters were away working, so it fell to her and a younger sister named Ethel to take care of the younger boys still at home.

Sanger soon tired of being a household drudge and being subjected to her father's dictatorial ways. Since educational standards were less stringent in those days, she had already done a short stint at teaching young children in New Jersey. She apparently did not care for this type of career, however, for she now set her sights on nursing. By 1900, Sanger was enrolled in a new nursing school in White Plains, New York. At the time, student nurses worked long hours at menial pursuits, while the academic requirements were less demanding than current curricula. Sanger seems to have been particularly interested in obstetrics. Although she did not receive the diploma normally gained at the end of three years, she had sufficient training to work as a sort of practical nurse. A photo of Sanger while she was in training shows a very attractive young woman; friends have remarked about her beautiful red hair and noted that she had green eyes.

The young woman's ambition to complete the three-year course was thwarted by a handsome architect named William Sanger, who was six years her senior. The child of German Jews, he had been brought to the United States while still a preschooler. In some ways he resembled her father, Michael Higgins. Both immigrants were idealists who stood for social justice, both were impractical dreamers, and both were opposed to organized religion. They took to one another when they first met.

Margaret and Bill, as he was known, were married in 1902. At first she did not announce the fact at the hospital, which forbade student nurses to marry. She had fully intended to complete the three-year course, but she soon gave in to her husband and resigned from the school of nursing before she finished.

The young couple rented an apartment in Manhattan. Their first child, Stuart, was born in 1903. Tuberculosis, which had first appeared when Margaret Sanger was at White Plains, became exacerbated during her pregnancy. Bill sent her to the well-known Trudeau Sanitarium at Saranac Lake. Antibiotic treatment was of course unknown, but some cases seemed to respond to rest and good nutrition. After Stuart's birth, Margaret returned to the Adirondacks for several months, where the baby and its nurse accompanied her. Tuberculosis can be fatal, so Bill provided what was considered the best treatment available. Apparently Margaret did not do well on the prescribed regimen and was advised to reenter the sanitarium. Instead, she traveled against advice to New York City with baby and nurse in tow. Bill rose to the occasion, and she gradually improved.

The Sangers moved to Hastings-on-Hudson, where they lived in a rented house while they were building their own. Margaret's illness had been costly, and there were many added expenses with the new home. Bill overextended himself, determined that his architectural dream would be a source of enjoyment to the family.

By 1908 the dream house was finally ready for occupancy, and the Sangers moved in. That night a fire destroyed furnishings and some of the structure. Although repairs were made, Margaret appeared to lose interest in the house that had been such an investment of Bill's talent and effort.

Three years later a second son, Grant, was born; then in 1911 a girl they called Peggy. Margaret soon tired of suburban life and persuaded Bill to move back to New York City. He reluctantly sold his property, striking a poor bargain.

Bill's widowed mother moved in with them, providing a reliable built-in babysitter. This freed Margaret to take some cases with Lillian Wald's Henry House visiting nurses and elsewhere. The young mother valued the opportunity to be out of the house and into the "real" world; her work also brought in some much-needed income.

In her autobiographical *My Fight for Birth Control*, Margaret Sanger describes some of the conditions she saw in the tenements:

> Women whose weary, pregnant, shapeless bodies refuse to accommodate themselves to the husbands' desires find husbands looking with lustful eyes upon other women, sometimes upon their own little daughters, six or seven years of age.

> The menace of another pregnancy hung like a sword over the head of every poor woman I came in contact with that year. The question which met me was always the same: What can I do to keep from it? or, What can I do to get out of this?

> Life for them had but one choice: either to abandon themselves to incessant childbearing, or to terminate their pregnancies through abortions.

Sanger's writings stated that family limitation by means of coitus interruptus or by use of the condom was often practiced by enlightened men. (Statistics showed that among the more affluent, the birth rate was falling.) She also made it clear that these methods were not practical for women in the slums, and she implied that a method under the woman's control was sorely needed.

Because a cure for tuberculosis was never certain, it is likely that Sanger had a personal interest in finding such a method, and it was in this period of her life that the death of Sadie Sachs made such a profound impression upon her. Whether Sadie Sachs really existed has been questioned. Perhaps she was a composite of various women Sanger saw. It makes little difference because Sadie's situation was common and also strikingly similar to one described by Emma Goldman.

There were many radicals among the Sangers' friends— freethinkers and agnostics. These radicals included John Reed, journalist and author of *Ten Days That Shook the World*; Bill Haywood, the labor organizer of the Industrial Workers of the World (IWW); Walter Lippmann, the editor who later became a famous author; Elizabeth Gurley Flynn of the IWW, Emma Goldman, and Alexander Berkman. Bill and Margaret joined Local 5 of the city's Socialist Party. Margaret occupied herself for a time recruiting members and writing for *The Call*, a Socialist paper. Her column entitled "What Every Girl Should Know" ran in 1912 and 1913. She dealt with pregnancy, abortion, menstruation, masturbation, and similar topics. Comstock banned a column that dealt with syphilis, but it appeared a few weeks later.

In 1912 textile workers in Lawrence, Massachusetts, went on strike because of a pay cut. The IWW became involved, and to enlist support, some children were removed to New York to stay in homes where they would be well cared for. Sanger helped with the "evacuation" and, in the role of a nurse, testified before a Congressional committee about the condition of the children. A pay raise was granted. The experience gave Sanger insight into the organization of such tactics; it also brought her some national recognition and friendships with Haywood and Flynn.

Margaret Sanger and her children spent the summer of 1913 on Cape Cod, with Bill coming from New York when he could. Ethel Byrne, a divorced sister, provided babysitting. Goldman and Berkman, as well as Haywood, were in Provincetown, and Sanger was able to spend a considerable amount of time with them.

The influence of these friends and other radicals Sanger met in New York was considerable. She came to embrace free love and that summer had a lover. He was one of many to come. She was discreet about such affairs, however, in contrast to Emma Goldman, who made no effort to pretend she was what some considered respectable. Bill did not believe in free love, however, and once declared, "I am essentially a monogamist."

But although her politics had veered to the left, Sanger felt strongly that socialists expended so much effort to overcome wage slavery that they neglected the problem of women's sex slavery. She had not forgotten Sadie Sachs and her own resolve to do something for such women.

With the children left in the care of their aunt, Sanger took the boat to Boston, particularly to look for medical information on contraception. She found very little information, however. It has been pointed out that a substantial body of knowledge was in print. It was not readily accessible to even the educated lay person, however, and if this knowledge were to be used widely, attitudes would have to be changed and laws revised. Sanger had much to do before she could help the Sadie Sachses of the world.

Opportunity soon presented itself. Bill Sanger was apparently an artist at heart and was becoming more interested in painting than in architecture. When his mother died in September 1913, he decided to go to Paris to study. Margaret saw that this would be an opportunity for her to learn about the contraceptive methods that appeared to keep the French birth rate low.

Details of the Sanger family's finances are sometimes lacking. Margaret's biographer, Ellen Chesler, writes that Margaret resented Bill's lack of responsibility. Family and friends seem to have helped, and on the whole, Margaret and the children appear to have lacked little. The latter, for instance, were often placed in good boarding schools (which action, incidentally, freed Sanger to follow her desires). It is difficult to separate her personal activities from those on behalf of her cause, but the philosophy she stated in *My Fight for Birth Control* gives the reader some insight.

> [Questions about financing a trip such as the one to Paris] always annoy me. . . . I don't really know how most of my ventures in this

work were ever financed. I am of no economical turn of mind. I do things first, and somehow or another, they get paid for. If I had waited to finance my various battles for birth control, I do not suppose they ever would have become realities. I suppose here is the real difference between the idealist—or the "fanatic," as we are called—and the ordinary "normal" human being.

Smaller families were in vogue in France after the Napoleonic Code provided that children share equally in a father's estate, rather than the inheritance going to the eldest son. With help from French labor leaders, Sanger looked into how families remained small and found that, despite the Catholic church, French mothers passed on to their daughters information about tampons, suppositories, and douches and regarded their forumlas as favorite recipes. French law imposed no Comstock-like restrictions; moreover, abortion was legal and performed by surgeons.

Aside from questions about the morality of abortion, many people of the era did not condone it. The chief risks were infection and hemorrhage. Obviously abortion was safer under a qualified surgeon than a lay midwife, but in the absence of antibiotics and modern blood banks, the patient was at considerable risk.

Less than three months after she had sailed for France, Margaret Sanger returned to New York with the children. Bill stayed to pursue his painting, as he had planned. This was really the end of the marriage. Margaret wanted out, but Bill was still in love with her. Divorce was not easily obtained, and in Margaret's case, did not come for some eight years.

Sanger's articles for *The Call* had been sufficiently popular to inspire her to write more. She decided to start a magazine aimed at stimulating working women to think for themselves. Her publication, *The Woman Rebel*, would defy Comstock by providing information on sexuality and contraception. Through her connections she found several hundred subscribers. She also had offers of free help in the production end.

Around this time, Sanger began to use the term *birth control*. Biographers Madeline Gray and Ellen Chesler disagree about who was the originator of the term, but as one colleague put it, "Without [Margaret], birth control would never have become household words."

The first issue of the new magazine appeared in March 1914. A woman rebel claimed "The right to be lazy. The right to be an unmarried mother. The right to destroy. The right to create. The right to live. The right to love." It was clear that editorial policy advocated birth control, and there was a promise of advice on birth control at a later date.

From the beginning, the U.S. Post Office objected to the magazine, warning that Sanger would face prosecution. In August she was arrested on four counts, the first three for violating Comstock regulations and the fourth for inciting murder and assassination. The latter charge was based on an article written by a contributor who subscribed to the anarchist belief that assassination of despots and their like was justified because it would help the masses. (Emma Goldman, when she was young, upheld such action.) Sanger's associates were radicals who were not all solely interested in women's reproductive rights, and she for a short time embraced some of their ideas. It was somewhat reckless of her as an editor, however, to accept such an article, even if she believed the magazine was protected by the Constitution's First Amendment guarantee. She was responsible and had to take the consequences.

Appearing in court without a lawyer, Sanger was given six weeks to prepare for her trial. She had the impression, however, that she would be given longer if that should become necessary.

Preparing no defense, Sanger instead used the time to write a pamphlet entitled *Family Limitation*. Responses to *The Woman Rebel* had convinced her of the urgent need for contraceptive information. Employing the facts she had learned in France, she used language aimed at ordinary people to talk about withdrawal, condoms, tampons, suppositories, and douches, presenting pros and cons. She also mentioned the type of pessary used in Europe. "It is the big battalions of unwanted babies that make life so hard for the working woman and keep her in poverty and stress from generation to generation," she wrote.

Finding a printer for the illegal venture was not easy. A courageous individual named Bill Shatoff, working in secret after hours, ran off 100,000 copies. The IWW locals and other groups had arranged for distribution and were waiting directions as to when this would be. The cost of the pamphlet was low, but it would bring the author some money.

October was upon her before Sanger had done anything about her case. When she asked for more time, her request was denied. Now she had to make serious decisions. Bill Sanger had just returned to the United States, so she would have to depend on him, a devoted father, to see to the children's welfare. She hurriedly made preparations to flee to Canada, then on to England, although that country was already involved in the First World War. In Canada Sanger managed to get a passport issued to her under an alias. After her ship set sail from Montreal to Liverpool, she sent a cable that released the copies as planned. At last her chosen mission had been launched, thanks largely to the financial and moral support of her radical friends.

In Liverpool, Sanger became acquainted with a radical Spaniard who was teaching at the university there. They soon became lovers, and she made a seven-week tour of Spain with him. Perhaps they would have married, but unfortunately this man died of tuberculosis in 1917.

Towards the end of November 1914, Sanger arrived in London. She contacted Dr. C. V. Drysdale of the neo–Malthusian movement. His ideas were not in vogue at the time, so he and his aged mother, Dr. Alice Vickery, were more than pleased to find an enthusiastic cohort. They helped Sanger in many ways, one being to provide an introduction to Havelock Ellis, the noted English psychologist and author. The fact that the first volume of his series, *Psychology of Sex*, had been banned on charges of obscenity may have created an immediate bond between Ellis and Sanger. At any rate, there was mutual attraction although Ellis was about 20 years older than Sanger. Very soon he became her mentor, guiding her study for a short time at the British Museum. Although he was her lover, his greatest influence on her was intellectual, and she maintained this type of contact with him until his death in 1939.

Early in 1915, with the encouragement of the Drysdales, Sanger visited a birth control clinic in the Hague. There, under Dr. Johannes Rutgers, she learned how to fit diaphragms and also how to give women individual advice about contraception.

Sanger had hoped to meet Dr. Aletta Jacobs in Amsterdam. This famous doctor had read in 1883 about Dr. Mensigna's spring diaphragm and then communicated with him about it. He had sent samples that soon convinced Jacobs of the device's safety and usefulness. She was familiar with the desire of many mothers who brought their infants to a free clinic: they wanted to avert pregnancy in the near future. To these women Dr. Jacobs offered the Mensigna pessary, as it was called. Eventually more than 50 contraceptive clinics were set up in the Netherlands. Supported by the Dutch Neo-Malthusian League, they operated at a low cost.

Dr. Jacobs considered Sanger a lay person and would not see her. Years later, at the Malthusian and Birth Control Conference in New York in 1925, Dr. Jacobs explained to Sanger, who had organized that conference, that she had erroneously assumed Sanger was promoting contraceptive devices as a commercial enterprise and had therefore refused to meet the nurse.

While Sanger was still in Europe, her husband had been tricked into giving an alleged friend of his wife a copy of *Family Limitation*. The friend turned out to be one of Comstock's decoys, and Bill was arrested. The case was deferred until the fall of 1915; when it came to trial, Bill chose 30 days in jail rather than the payment of a $150 fine.

For reasons that can only be guessed, Sanger decided it was time to return to face trial herself and she arrived in New York in October. Her presence in Europe had been beneficial from the standpoint of the birth control cause. She had made many valuable contacts, including Marie Stopes, the subject of the next chapter.

Soon after Sanger's return, her daughter Peggy died of pneumonia, then often a fatal disease. This was a blow from which Sanger never recovered. Bill, too, was inconsolable, and Grant, who was close to Peggy's age, was deeply affected.

Sanger's trial was postponed more than once and finally ended in February 1917. Much had changed since she had fled the country. For a number of reasons, she and her cause were now more in the public eye, and the public was more receptive to both.

Bill Sanger's trial had received some publicity. When the

presiding judge made remarks about society being better off if Christian women would have children rather than wasting time on woman suffrage, feminists were angry and others felt new sympathy for those who advocated birth control.

When Margaret Sanger was occupied taking care of the critically ill Peggy, the public realized that the crusading Mrs. Sanger was also a mother. The child's death was something with which many parents of that day could identify.

Before her self-created exile, Sanger had planned for what later evolved into the National Birth Control League. During her absence, Mary Ware Dennett, the subject of Chapter 6, became influential in this group. Dennett and Sanger did not often see eye-to-eye, but just before the trial, the National Birth Control League announced that it was behind Sanger.

Dr. Marie Stopes, at Sanger's request, had been instrumental in obtaining British support. An open letter to President Wilson condemned criminal prosecution of Sanger because she had circulated material that most civilized countries accepted. The letter was signed by Stopes herself and other prominent persons such as H. G. Wells and Arnold Bennett.

Family Limitation had been very well received, and Sanger continued to revise it when necessary. Clearly, many women desperately wanted birth control.

The Bradlaugh-Besant case had made the British public more receptive to the birth control issue; the publicity involving Sanger's trial had the same effect on the American public. Sanger was determined to refuse the service of any lawyer whose aim was to obtain her acquittal through a promise that she would not break the law in the future. She intended to challenge the law.

In the end, all charges were dropped. The *New York Sun* wrote of "a prosecutor loath to prosecute and a defendant anxious to be tried." Sanger was free. But even though Comstock had just died, his law and those based on it still stood.

Sanger took advantage of the situation to publicize the birth control movement from Boston to Los Angeles by delivering her basic lecture many times during a ten-day period. At first, public speaking made her nervous, but she did well at it and was adroit at changing her delivery to appeal to specific audiences. Over the years, people cited her ability to stimulate real enthusiasm for her cause. Eventually she commanded reasonable remuneration for her lectures.

Socially prominent women who leaned towards feminism were showing interest in Sanger. (As far back as when the Sangers first moved to New York, heiress Mabel Dodge, for example, had taken a great fancy to Sanger.) Especially gifted as a fund raiser, Sanger began increasingly to look for support to the upper and middle classes rather than to radicals. She knew that birth control was just one interest of the latter, while it was her prime focus. Haywood himself had once spoken about the day when working people would have enough money to have as many children as they wanted. Sanger was emphatic that the choice of the number of children a woman would bear and raise was hers alone; if she wanted one, so be it, even if her husband wanted six. Apparently this message was not important to the IWW.

Influenced by what she had seen in the Netherlands, Sanger decided to open a birth control clinic. She picked the Brownsville area of Brooklyn for its location. Her sister Ethel Byrne, a registered nurse, assisted her, and Fania Mindell, a recent Chicago recruit, also volunteered to help. They rented a tenement location and had the following handbills printed in English, Yiddish, and Italian:

MOTHERS!
Can you afford to have a large family?
Do you want any more children?
If not, why do you have them?
DO NOT KILL. DO NOT TAKE LIFE, BUT PREVENT.
Safe Harmless Information can be obtained of trained
Nurses at
46 AMBOY STREET
Near Pitkin Ave. — Brooklyn

Tell Your Friends and Neighbors   All Mothers Welcome
A registration fee of 10 cents entitles any mother to this
information.

At the end of the opening day, October 16, 1916, 140 women had been seen, proving the effectiveness of the handbills. Because of

Margaret Sanger, 1916
Courtesy of the Planned Parenthood
Federation of America, Inc.

these handbills, Yiddish and Italian newspapers had publicized the opening of America's first birth control clinic, with the result that women came from as far away as Massachusetts.

The clinic provided each client with information. The Mizpah pessary, used to treat prolapse of the uterus, was also a contraceptive and was available from drug stores. Although they were nurses, the sisters did not fit these devices but estimated from a woman's obstetric history the size of pessary required.

On the ninth day that the clinic was open, a policewoman posed as a client. The next afternoon, the vice squad arrested Sanger and Mindell and confiscated records and other materials. The two women spent the night in a filthy jail before they were released on bail. They reopened the clinic, and again the police closed it down. Byrne had been absent when the others were arrested, but now she was served with a warrant.

As she awaited trial, Sanger had sympathizers among the poor women she had helped in the past and among the affluent women whom she was now beginning to court. The latter included the National Birth Control League's Committee of 100. Mary Dennett was a member; also the Chicago heiress Juliet Rublee and philanthropist Gertrude Pinchot. Pinchot had previously paid school tuition for two of the Sanger children.

Ethel Byrne was the first to be sentenced on January 22, 1917. Convicted of breaking Section 1142 of New York State's penal code, a "little Comstock law" that prohibited giving contraceptive advice for any reason, she was sent to the workhouse on Blackwell's Island for 30 days.

Using a tactic of the British suffragettes, Byrne went on a hunger strike. She even refused liquids, and after 103 hours the authorities ordered force feeding through a stomach tube. Although there was important war news to cover, newspapers throughout the country reported on Byrne's progress; this was exactly the type of publicity that Sanger welcomed. Franklin P. Adams of the *New York Tribune* wrote prophetically that "it will be hard to make the youth of 1967 believe that in 1917 a woman was imprisoned for doing what Mrs. Byrne did." On January 29 the Committee of 100 staged a protest rally at Carnegie Hall. This rally not only raised money but brought additional exposure.

As Byrne grew progressively weaker, Sanger agreed, on behalf of her sister, to a pardon from the governor of New York, on the condition that Byrne would promise to abide by the law. This condition of course precluded her participation in future activities that she would probably have wanted to join.

Mindell was charged with selling Sanger's *What Every Girl Should Know* and fined $50. On appeal, this decision was reversed. Charged with maintaining a public nuisance, Sanger was also convicted of breaking Section 1142. Her lawyer was Jonah Goldstein, a protégé of Lillian Wald. Refusing a fine, she had to spend 30 days in a Queens prison. (Blackwell's Island did not want Ethel Byrne's sister.) Most of Sanger's fellow-prisoners were drug addicts or prostitutes; she felt compassion for both groups.

Goldstein had appealed Sanger's case, and a verdict came early in 1918, after she had already been released from prison. The judge upheld her conviction under Section 1142. Section 1145 allowed physicians to prescribe contraception for the cure or prevention of disease. This did not exonerate Sanger, who was not a physician, but it was Goldstein's intent to test Section 1145. Much to Sanger's satisfaction, the judge's interpretation was that the section applied to conditions other than venereal diseases. So now doctors in the court's jurisdiction were at liberty to provide contraception to patients with heart problems, tuberculosis, and other diseases.

Sanger was now devoting much time to a publication named *Birth Control Review*. The editorial board included the socialist leader and pacifist Eugene Debs, Havelock Ellis, C. V. Drysdale, Johannes Rutgers, Marie Stopes, and other notables friendly with Sanger. Her *Family Limitation* was still being distributed to disadvantaged women. In February she spent three months in California writing her first book, *Women and the New Race*. In this work she lauded her sister, Ethel Byrne, writing: "No single act of self-sacrifice in the history of the birth-control movement has done more to awaken the conscience of the public or to arouse the courage of women." Highly successful, *Women* was followed by several more books. Sanger was fortunate in having good editors who gave her much aid.

With the European war over, Sanger spent considerable time in England, where the Drysdales arranged lectures for her. Always a devotee of Ellis, she was also influenced by H. G. Wells, the famous British author. He was another of her lovers, but also a genuine admirer of her work.

Sanger had found an American publisher for Marie Stopes's

Married Love, though the result was an expurgated version. The two women did not continue a friendship, however; Stopes was closer to Mary Dennett.

Sanger visited Germany in search of information on a contraceptive jelly. There she found that large families were being encouraged in order to make up for war losses. (France was pursuing the same policy.) A pacifist, Sanger believed that a surplus population tended to provoke war. She was saddened to see these countries repeat past mistakes.

While in England, Sanger underwent surgery to remove some tissue near the tonsils. She had been plagued with tuberculosis for years, and with the removal of this focus of infection she would be cured.

At first Sanger had objected to contraceptive control being in the hands of the medical profession. She had been repelled when a German physician told her that in his country the doctors, not the women involved, decided who would and who would not have abortions. Sanger felt that the control of reproduction was a social, not a medical matter, but she came to support physician control because she realized that the birth control movement would not progress without it. The immediate problem was that most doctors were still reluctant to make contraception available, especially to the poor. There were restrictive laws to contend with, and the profession seemed in no hurry to contest them. In New York State, even with the favorable 1918 decision on Section 1045, there had been little progress.

Sanger planned the First American Birth Control Conference, held in New York in November 1921. Those invited included some dignitaries attending the Washington Naval Disarmament Conference and also members of the American Public Health Association. Sanger used the occasion to ask physicians to support her; she also announced her plan to open a birth control clinic run under physician management. This conference was interrupted by a police raid, which elicited extensive press coverage. (Some police raids associated with Sanger's activities were promoted by the Catholic church.)

While Sanger had been abroad, Mary Dennett's name had been before the public as an advocate of birth control. The police raid notwithstanding, the conference showed that now Margaret Sanger, not Mary Dennett, was the real leader of the birth control movement. Sanger was very adroit at organizing such affairs, and there would be many more to come.

In 1922 Sanger incorporated the American Birth Control League under the laws of the state of New York. The American League replaced the National League, which in 1919 had become the Voluntary Parenthood League. The latter was defunct by 1924.

That year Sanger and her son Grant, then 13, visited the Orient. Baroness Shidzue Ishimoto, later referred to as the Japanese Margaret Sanger, had been in New York, where she became aware of Sanger's work. Realizing that birth control would help young Japanese women, she had a liberal group in her country sponsor a series of lectures by Sanger. Later Sanger and her son traveled to Korea, China, Hong Kong, Singapore, Ceylon, Egypt, Italy, France, and England. In London, Sanger attended the Fifth International Neo-Malthusian Conference. Her wanderings and lectures occupied most of a year.

Besides her son Grant, Sanger was accompanied by Noah Slee, who had made a fortune as the founder of the Three-in-One Oil Company. He was 18 years older than Sanger and inclined to be conservative. They were married in London in September 1922. Slee was exceedingly generous and built a beautiful house in Fishkill, New York, as a wedding gift for Sanger. He not only provided her with all sorts of material benefits but undertook the education of Stuart and Grant, both of whom became physicians. His largesse extended to other relatives and friends of Sanger.

Her new husband's support for her work was very important to Sanger. They led independent lives, Sanger coming and going as she pleased. Slee donated thousands of dollars to the birth control cause and his business expertise was a valuable asset to the movement.

On returning to the United States, Sanger involved herself in making the permanent clinic she had envisioned materialize. Financed by a British Malthusian named Clinton Chance, it was named the Clinical Research Bureau. (Note the absence of the term *birth control*.) Dr. Dorothy Bocker was hired for the first year.

No public promotion was done; patients simply heard about the clinic by word of mouth.

Not satisfied with Dr. Bocker's performance, Sanger engaged on a part-time basis, without pay, Dr. Hannah Stone, a pediatrician aged 32. Picking Dr. Stone, who would later be a coauthor of the best-seller *A Marriage Manual,* was a master stroke. During her first year, Dr. Stone found more than 1600 women who needed contraception for what she considered health reasons. She kept excellent records and saw that cases were followed up when the women failed to return to the clinic. But this courageous woman paid a price for her affiliation with birth control: she had to relinquish her staff privileges at the lying-in section of New York Hospital and for some years was not accepted for membership in the New York Academy of Medicine. Regarding her commitment to birth control, she said, "It needs some of us who care."

Despite its name, the American Birth Control League was for some time far from national in scope. Naturally the New York League was most active and served as a model for what could be done. Gradually a network of affiliates grew up. Sanger's lectures inspired the establishment of new affiliates to work at the local level or the renewal of some that were inactive. The volunteers in the movement were typically white American upper- or middle-class women. Success in starting and maintaining clinics depended on various factors. State laws differed, the Catholic church was more influential in some areas than in others, and funding varied. In nearly all clinics, however, the law was being circumvented in one way or another. Sometimes because of the legal situation, sometimes because of society's disapproval, most volunteers showed considerable courage to be part of the birth control movement.

The medical profession became more receptive when Sanger hired Dr. James Cooper to proselytize for contraception. For a period of four years, this former medical missionary visited medical societies and individual physicians to acquaint them with birth control methods. Sponsored by the American Birth Control League of New York, he also encouraged support for local groups. Together with Dr. Stone, he developed a contraceptive jelly that was relatively cheap. Diaphragms, however, had to be smuggled into the country for some years. Slee, for one, later financed home manufacture.

The Sixth International Neo-Malthusian and Birth Control Conference in 1925 was an outstanding success, with more than 1000 delegates coming to New York. Dr. Stone's report on the clinic's research was very well received. According to her figures, the diaphragm when used with the lactic paste was 98 percent effective. The conference made a strong impression on Dr. Robert Dickinson, a noted gynecologist, and later he did much to make the medical community understand Sanger's crusade.

In 1937 the American Medical Association endorsed birth control. Twenty-five years had passed since its outgoing president, Dr. Abraham Jacobi, had urged such action.

Darwin's theory of natural selection had encouraged interest in eugenics. In 1908 the Eugenics Society was established. Frances Galton, its president, advocated "for the more suitable races or strains of blood a better chance of prevailing speedily over the less suitable." The word "fit" was sometimes used in place of "suitable," and even "rich" and "poor" were substituted.

During the 1920s, some proponents of eugenics joined the birth control movement. According to Sanger, "The eugenicists wanted to shift the birth control emphasis from fewer children for the poor to more children for the rich. We went back of that and sought first to stop the multiplication of the unfit." She certainly advocated the latter—not an unusual stance, since many states had compulsory sterilization laws for conditions such as insanity, feeblemindedness, and inherited or transmissible disease. (At that time, less was known about such conditions than is known today.)

Advocates of birth control, Sanger included, have been accused of prejudice in cases when minorities such as Jews or blacks were a large part of the poor or immigrant population to whom contraception was offered. With regard to more children for the rich, Sanger's position was that if each woman could choose the number of her children, that number would usually be small.

Besides the official opposition of the Catholics, Sanger had to contend with some members of other denominations who refused to compromise on the literal wording of Scripture; these people also tended to oppose the freedom that birth control would afford women. Some people feared that contraception would be used by the unmarried. Others believed that children were the only joy of the poor, who should not be discouraged from having them. Carrie Chapman Catt, the woman suffrage leader, represented the opinion of some women when she suggested that advocacy of contraception be combined with equally strong propaganda for continence. "No animal is so uncontrolled as is the mass of men," she wrote privately to Sanger.

Despite the roadblocks, the idea of using birth control gradually became palatable to many. In 1931 a published report noted that millions of Protestants, as well as a conference of American rabbis, agreed that the sex act, without relation to procreation, was morally right. Mary Dennett, for a short period, helped to keep the issue before the public. The Depression was an ally of contraception, for many were forced to practice it, whether or not they desired more offspring. More than half the states had birth control leagues by 1935, and some 300 clinics existed.

In 1928 Sanger had resigned as president of the American Birth Control League, and a year later she withdrew from its membership. She did not always agree with what was being done, and now it was time to let others exert their influence. She retained control of the clinic, however, which was separated from the League and was the recipient of large donations from Slee. It continued until the 1970s as a highly successful venture that not only provided women with contraceptive services and counseling but also made available valuable medical and scientific data.

For years Sanger was involved in lobbying for federal legislation that would nullify the Comstock Law as it applied to medical practice.

Her efforts were in vain until 1937. Section 305 of the Revenue Act barred importation of contraceptives, and such materials mailed to Dr. Stone (for a test case) had been seized. The defense lawyer was the very able Morris Ernst. When the case reached the Circuit Court of Appeals, Judge Augustus Hand upheld the previous opinion of the Federal District Court of Southern New

York that there should be no interference with "doctors prescribing for the health of the people." He added that Section 305 and similar statutes originated in the Comstock Law. Then he said: "Its design, in our opinion, was not to prevent the importation, sale or carriage by mail of things which might intelligently be employed by conscientious and competent physicians for the purpose of saving life or promoting the well-being of their patients."

The Comstock Law was now substantially weakened. Connecticut and Massachusetts, however, still had very restrictive laws about contraceptives. It was not until 1965 that these laws were removed by a Supreme Court decision that made contraception a legal right of married Americans. Five years later, Congress rewrote the federal Comstock law. In 1972 the Supreme Court insured that unmarried persons were entitled to contraception. During the 1960s, federal funding for effective family planning programs became a reality; Sanger had pushed for this for many years.

In 1939, Sanger rejoined the American Birth Control League, taking the role of honorary president. In 1942 the organization's name was changed to the Planned Parenthood Federation of America, and she is rightly considered its founder.

From an early stage of her career, Sanger grasped the dangers of excessive global population growth and visited countries all over the world to encourage the use of birth control. Appropriately, the organization she started now works outside the United States through the International Planned Parenthood Federation and Family Planning International Assistance.

Retirement brought Sanger time to pursue such hobbies as painting and to spend time with her grandchildren. She also retained her interest in birth control. Although she appeared to favor the diaphragm, she was always interested in research on new and better methods. As shall be discussed in Chapter 8, she played a role in financing the development of the anovulant pill, but she did not live to see abortion legalized in 1973 through *Roe v. Wade*.

Noah Slee died in 1943. Sanger outlived him by 23 years, dying in Tucson, Arizona, her home for many years.

During her lifetime, Margaret Sanger received many honors and awards. After her death, she was paid an outstanding tribute by historian James Reed, author of *From Private Vice to Public Virtue*: "Through [her] achievements she had a greater impact on the world than any other American woman."

Chapter 5

Marie Stopes

Motherhood should be voluntary and guided by the best
scientific knowledge available.
— Inscription on wall of
Stopes-Roe Mothers' Clinic, 1921

Marie Stopes, who was British, could not claim to be the
founder of the world's first birth control clinic—that honor
belongs to Dr. Jacobs. But Dr. Stopes does have a genuine first.
In 1927 she organized a birth control clinic that operated from a
horse-drawn mobile van; it made its first stop near the public
library in Bethnal Green.

On October 15, 1880, in Edinburgh, Scotland, Marie
Charlotte Carmichael Stopes became the first child born to Henry
and Charlotte (Carmichael) Stopes. Charlotte was an advocate of
woman suffrage; she was also a bluestocking, the first Scottish
woman to take a university certificate. (Degrees were not yet
granted to women.) Her husband, 11 years younger, supported
her activities. An educated man, his consuming interest was ar-
chaeology. He was apparently an architect but had important
connections with the brewing industry. Charlotte Stopes's image
as a Shakespearian scholar and as a feminist made a deep impression on her firstborn. Marie idolized her father, and at a young
age was thoroughly familiar with his valuable collection of
prehistoric instruments. The family moved from Edinburgh to
London when Marie was an infant. She lived close to London for
most of the rest of her life. A second daughter was born four years

later, and in time it became Marie Stopes's lot to support that sister until the latter's death at 38.

When she was 12, Stopes was sent back to Edinburgh to school, and two years later she attended the North London Collegiate School. Although she did not distinguish herself academically, she read widely. For as long as she could remember, she had helped her father search for rocks at their summer home in Kent. Her interest in Darwin's writings shocked a maternal aunt, who was horrified when Henry even mentioned the scientist's name before a young girl.

Henry Stopes, a Quaker, left the religious upbringing of his daughter to his wife, Charlotte, a member of the Free Church of Scotland. Charlotte was more tolerant than most Victorian mothers, but it should be remembered that religion was a vital part of life at this time. Stopes herself said, "I was brought up in the rigours of the stern Scottish old-fashioned Presbyterianism, in which hell was presented as an absolute reality which I stood in imminent danger of inheriting; special books were kept for Sunday reading; no toys were allowed on Sundays, when Bible chapters and texts had to be learnt as well as church attendances fulfilled."

Although her parents wanted her to go to a women's college, Stopes enrolled at 19 in University College in London. She had picked this school because women could study there under distinguished scientists and also receive degrees. She worked extremely hard and after only two years, obtained the bachelor of science degree with first class honors in botany and third class honors in geology. Her record was better than that of any male student, and her work justified the confidence of a male professor who had accepted her despite a previously mediocre record.

Stopes's father died in 1902, leaving her mother and her with the responsibility for the family—a responsibility that would become more burdensome to Stopes as time passed.

Her academic success had brought Stopes a scholarship to study for a year on the Continent. Knowing that she needed extra training before such a venture, she first spent an additional year at University College.

Stopes's botanical research centered on reproduction in a

seed-bearing species known as the cycads. At Munich there was an authority on this subject—Professor K. Goebel, who had an important collection of both living and petrified forms. To date, no woman had received a degree in botany from the University of Munich, but this state of affairs did not deter Stopes. Impressed with the ability of his student, Professor Goebel soon made arrangements for her to work toward a Ph.D. Because her German was poor, she was assigned to someone to help her with the writing of her thesis. The research went well, due to her native ability, enthusiasm, and capacity for sustained hard work. When the year was over, she was Dr. Marie Stopes.

Stopes found time for some pleasure too. She enjoyed Munich's art collection, she heard Wagnerian operas, and she once saw Isadora Duncan dance. Incidentally, Stopes scorned the Prussian military; she refused to step into the gutter when an officer passed. At the university, she was an attractive female among thousands of males. Stopes loved to dance and also to be part of the frequent gatherings in cafes. Even botanical expeditions to the Alps were fun. Through Professor Goebel she met scholars from various parts of the world and fell in love with one, a Japanese.

Kenjiro Fujii was 37 and an assistant professor at the Imperial University in Tokyo. His interest in the reproductive process of the gingko tree impressed Stopes, but she was also aware that he had a wife and small daughter in Japan.

From the research standpoint, Stopes would have liked to remain longer under Professor Goebel. But since she was now destined to be the chief provider for her family, she could not afford to do that. Instead, in 1904, at the age of 24, she took a position at Manchester University as a junior lecturer and demonstrator. The first woman to have the appointment, she lectured successfully and at the same time worked towards a degree of doctor of science at London University.

While at Manchester, which was near coal mines, Stopes became interested in what are somtimes called coal balls—masses of petrified plant material embedded in coal seams. Sir Jethro Teall, then director of the Geological Survey, heard Stopes lecture on coal. "I went to encourage a young girl," he remarked, "and I remained to learn from a master." Stopes never lost her interest in coal, publishing widely about it. For instance, her 1918 monograph entitled *The Constitution of Coal*, with R. W. Wheeler, was well known.

Instead of returning to Tokyo directly from Munich, Professor Fujii turned up in England, supposedly to study under Stopes's London mentor, Professor F. W. Oliver. Fujii's wife wanted to marry someone else and was seeking a divorce. Details of the Stopes-Fujii love affair, which lasted for five years, appeared in print in 1911 as *Love Letters of a Japanese*, by G. N. Mortlake. This was a pseudonym for Stopes herself, who edited the letters. How closely the letters reflected fact is not clear. Apparently there was no sexual involvement between the pair—Fujii was still technically married. But when he sailed for home in July 1905, they intended to marry.

With the divorce final in 1906, Stopes went to Japan in the summer of 1907. Her support came from the Royal Society—the first such help to be extended to a female investigator. She was to study samples from the island of Hokkaido that might shed light on the evolution of angiosperms, plants with seeds encased in an ovary. (Fujii had sent her such a sample in which she found an angiosperm—a fact that bolstered her grant application.)

In Tokyo, Stopes took advantage, when she could, of living as a Japanese rather than as an Englishwoman. The food and attire were to her liking.

For the exploration of Hokkaido, Stopes had an interpreter as well as guides and laborers—all males. Travel in the island was difficult because of forests and swollen rivers. Tall sasa—somewhat like bamboo—proved a real impediment, but Stopes was an outdoors person, accustomed to roughing it. For example, in the summer of 1906, she and the sole female professor in Norway made an expedition that brought them to the Arctic circle by way of the Lofoten Islands. But the terrain in Hokkaido challenged the young British paleobotanist, as she wrote in her diary:

> Without a couple of my escorts to put their feet to make steps, or
> to give a hand round corners, I could not get along at all. . . . In
> crossing a river we all kept hands . . . how the loaded coolies could
> manage I cannot imagine. It was only the feeling that as I was the

leader I daren't show fright, that kept me going over some of those places. However, we were well rewarded, for the fossils we got that afternoon were the best obtained so far, and after several hours' brilliant sunshine the water perceptibly lessened.

These field explorations lasted about two and a half weeks.

Although her presence in Japan had brought Stopes academic success, she sensed that Fujii's attitude towards her had changed. He claimed illness: its nature—whether physical or mental—was not clear, but something was awry. He also mentioned the possibility that he had picked up leprosy (that would manifest itself later). Stopes finally decided that Fujii did not intend to marry her. After a total stay of ten months in Japan, she sailed for England via Vancouver on January 24, 1908.

In 1911, Stopes met Canadian botanist Reginald Ruggles Gates at a gathering of scientists in St. Louis. Three months later they were married in Montreal. She was 31 and he two years younger. She kept her maiden name (under which she had published), a decision that was more unusual in 1911 than it is today.

The couple decided to live in England. Stopes now had an appointment at University College in London, her alma mater, while Gates became a lecturer in biology at the Medical School of St. Thomas Hospital.

Unfortunately, the marriage failed, and the couple parted after three years. While the divorce was pending, Stopes lived in a tent in Northumberland. In 1916 she obtained an annulment, medical examination having disclosed that she was still a virgin. According to her, Gates was impotent. Although this seems to have been the basic reason for the divorce, a third person was involved.

Alymer Maude was an author 22 years older than Stopes and was not living with his wife. Stopes and Gates had invited him to live in their Hampstead home because they liked him and welcomed the prospect of extra money from his board. Stopes's marriage was not going well, and she fell in love with Maude, but the affair remained platonic. Gates finally threw Maude out of the house. The latter became Stopes's biographer, omitting much and writing what she wanted. In 1926, Stopes dramatized the triangle in *Vectia*, stating that the play was autobiographical.

Married Love, the book that made Stopes famous, was published in 1918. Her preface stated: "In my own marriage I paid such a terrible price for sex-ignorance that I feel knowledge gained at such a cost should be placed at the service of humanity." (Stopes biographer June Rose doubts this ignorance.) Stopes's original plan, however, had been "to convey the help and knowledge in *Married Love*, not in a strong solution as it now is in one book, but diluted into a series of novels and romances. The first of these I drafted as a narrative interspersed with poems conveying one of the many facets of the subject through the medium of a tale." In 1911 she sent this first attempt to Maurice Hewlett for criticism; he was a novelist whom she admired.

Hewlett "recognized immediately its enthusiasm" but offered serious criticism. It was too short, there was no conclusion, the verses had no relation to the rest of the manuscript. His advice was to rewrite: "If your Ms., as it exists now, were my own, I should keep it by me until I felt a recurrence of the mood."

According to Stopes, as time passed, "I saw more and more clearly that what the world wanted was . . . help in some form, direct, swift and simple." According to U.S. District Court Judge J. W. Woolsey's opinion in 1931, what she produced was "a considered attempt to explain to married people how their mutual sex life may be made happier." Although the Victorian age was past, sex was seldom discussed publicly. Blackie and Son as well as Allen and Unwin having turned down *Married Love*, Stopes had trouble finding a publisher. A small house—A. C. Fifield— eventually took it on as a subsidized venture. For this project Stopes borrowed £200 from a rich man she had recently met.

An American edition was published simultaneously, thanks to the help of Margaret Sanger, who had met Stopes in the Fabian Hall in London in 1915. From Sanger's autobiography we learn:

> Later when I came back to the United States, I brought with me the manuscript of *Married Love*, and tried every established publisher in New York, receiving a rejection from each. Finally I induced Dr. William J. Robinson to publish it under the auspices of his *Critic and Guide*, a monthly magazine which took up many subjects the *Journal of the American Medical Association* would not touch.

Marie Stopes
Courtesy of the National Portrait Gallery, London

Unfortunately, even here the manuscript had to be expurgated. The Dr. Robinson referred to was the first American physician to demand that contraceptive knowledge be taught to medical students. By 1918 *Married Love* was banned from the mails because of the Comstock Law. It was legalized in 1931 by Judge Woolsey's decision and then published by Putnam.

The book was an immediate success in Britain. The postwar paper shortage presented Fifield with difficulties, but Stopes herself took part in the task of procuring an adequate supply. Eventually more than a million copies were sold. Translations appeared in many languages, including Arabic. In 1935, Edwin Weeks in *This Trade of Writing* ranked *Married Love* sixteenth out of the 25 most influential books written since 1885. Whether everything Stopes wrote was correct is beside the point; she succeeded in making people view sex in a different light. Without giving contraceptive information, she made it clear that in many circumstances, birth control was part of married love. In one passage, she noted the difference in attitudes in Holland and America:

> It is important to observe that Holland, the country which takes *most* care that children shall be well and voluntarily conceived, has increased its survival-rate, and has thereby, not diminished, but increased its population, and has the lowest infant mortality rate in Europe. While in America, where the outrageous "Comstock Laws" confuse wise scientific prevention with illegal abortion and label them both as "obscene," thus preventing people from obtaining decent hygenic knowledge, horrible and criminal abortion is more frequent than in any other country.

Countless readers of *Married Love* wrote to Stopes about their problems, and the majority of their questions involved birth control. Thus her crusade for effective sex education took a new turn. Her *Wise Parenthood* (1918) and *Contraception: Its Theory, History, and Practice* (1923) were answers to these questions.

The man who loaned Stopes money to subsidize the publication of *Married Love* was Humphrey Verdon Roe, who would soon become her husband. He had at first pursued a military career, fighting in the Boer War. His brother, Alliot, was an inventor who had great faith in the future of aviation. Humphrey left the army in 1902 to manage the family business, which manufactured men's suspenders. He invested heavily in his brother's interest, and together they formed a company that made the AVRO (for A. V. Roe and Company) biplane in 1910. With the advent of World War I, these planes were in great demand. As a result, Humphrey Roe became a rich man.

In 1917, Roe enlisted as a flyer. It was during this time that he met Stopes when he was sent home wounded to England. After breaking an engagement to another woman, he married Stopes that year; she was 37 and he 41.

As did Sanger's second husband, Noah Slee, Roe contributed generously to the cause of birth control. Even before he knew Stopes, he had tried to found a birth control clinic for the poor of Manchester, volunteering to give Manchester Hospital £1000 a year for five years and £12,000 when he died. In this endeavor he was encouraged and advised by Councillor Margaret Ashton, philanthropist and social worker. The offer was turned down due to the fear that the hospital would lose supporters who did not approve of birth control.

When the war was over, Roe and Stopes decided to devote themselves to public service. Stirred by her readers' ignorance of sexual matters, Stopes was ready to start a birth control clinic, an endeavor for which she had her husband's overwhelming support. Accordingly, Stopes resigned her lectureship at Universitiy College in 1920. Her prestige in science was considerable, but her permanent impact would be in the field of social work.

Stopes believed that the government-supported prenatal and child welfare clinics already in existence were well equipped to provide contraceptive services but lacked the will. Her target group was poor mothers, and with this in mind, Stopes and Roe founded the Mothers' Clinic in Holloway, a working-class area of North London. A qualified midwife saw the women, and a woman doctor was available for consultation. Services were free, and contraceptives were sold at a cost or provided free if women could not pay. Stopes stressed individual attention for each woman, with good record keeping. By far the most recommended device was the small high-domed rubber cervical cap. She felt that working women, in common with their middle-class and upper-class sisters, would accept birth control if it were made accessible to them, and she wanted to prove this.

Opposition to all aspects of birth control came of course from the Roman Catholic church and from others who thought that marriage existed for the procreation of children. The severe loss of life in the recent war was much in the public's mind and caused some to object to contraception. Opposition sometimes caused newspapers to decline to publicize Stopes's activities; even London Transport refused to display clinic advertisements.

Feeling that the clinic needed more publicity, Stopes organized a great public meeting at Queen's Hall in May 1921. Medical dignitaries, politicians, and of course Roe and Stopes spoke to a crowd in excess of 2000. Edward Cecil, the writer, recorded his impression of the meeting:

> It sometimes happens that one feels instinctively that an event in which one is sharing will become historic. I had that impression at the Queen's Hall Meeting on Constructive Birth Control. It requires some courage today to confess belief in birth control. To stand up for it is to invite abuse and be sure of getting it, but the day will come when parents will teach it to their children, and the State will recognize the necessity and wisdom of putting within the reach of all proper, practical knowledge on the control of conception. In that day the Queen's Hall will be looked back upon as historic. To my mind the saddest fact in the life of the people is the terrible lot of the women of the poor. They are slaves, and one of the ways in which they are slaves is that they are slaves of a kind of child-bearing which is no good to any one. Birth control would be the Magna Carta of the women of the poor.

A Malthusian League clinic was opened in November 1921 in Walworth, a slum area of London. Here Dr. Norman Haire was prone to recommend the Mensinga spring diaphragm. Stopes believed, apparently with little basis, that this was detrimental to the vaginal wall. (She was also anti–Semitic and disliked the Jewish Dr. Haire.) Because Stopes did not welcome another clinic over which she had no control, she offered no support. Malthusians were more interested in population and economic problems and less interested in personal concerns than Stopes, but other issues were involved in her attitude toward the group. The Malthusians revered the memory of Bradlaugh, and Stopes's reading had aroused in her an unreasonable dislike of Bradlaugh.

That same year, Stopes addressed a large meeting in New York's Town Hall that was sponsored by Mary Dennett's Voluntary Parenthood League. Margaret Sanger and Stopes seem to have regarded one another as rivals, and after their initial contacts, they steered clear of each other.

Sanger's feelings are revealed in a letter she wrote to one of her lovers, Hugh de Selincourt: she felt that Stopes's success in the birth control movement was due to Havelock Ellis, the Drysdales, and others, who were active long before Dr. Stopes appeared on the scene.

In 1923, when reformer Bertrand Russell requested Stopes's support in a case that involved Sanger's *Family Limitation* being regarded as obscene, the British birth control advocate refused him.

Stopes had her own legal battles. The best known was her suit against Dr. Halliday Sutherland, a convert to Roman Catholicism. (There is evidence that he had official backing from the church; Stopes was inclined, however, to suspect a Catholic conspiracy when none existed.) Sutherland had written in his 1922 book, *Birth Control: A Statement of Christian Doctrine Against the Neo-Malthusians*, that birth control was "exposing the poor to experiment." According to him, the Mothers' Clinic prescribed "a method of contraception described by [Anne Louise McIlroy, Professor of Obstetrics and Gynecology at the Royal Free Hospital] as 'the most harmful method of which I have had exposure.'" Stopes sued because of these statements, and the case dragged on, with appeals, for two years. Technically, she lost, and the costs involved were heavy. Nevertheless, the case brought welcome publicity to the birth control cause.

The medical profession was slowly being converted to the benefits of contraception. A great step forward was made when in 1921 the King's Physician, Lord Dawson of Penn, told an Anglican congress in Birmingham that "Birth control is here to stay." He made clear his belief that artificial means of contraception were desirable on medical, social, and personal grounds and called upon the church to support that stand.

The movement continued to grow. Stopes founded in 1923 the Society for Constructive Birth Control and Racial Progress. It aimed "to supply all who still need it with full knowledge of sound physiological methods of control." The society maintained that the Ministry of Health, not private enterprise, should provide contraceptive services to working-class women. It also stated that it was "just as much the aim of Constructive Birth Control to secure contraception of those married people who are healthy, childless and desire children, as it is to furnish security from conception to those who are radically diseased, already overburdened with children or in any way unfitted for parenthood."

The latter aim reflects the position of the eugenicists, and Stopes certainly subscribed to their ideas. In many ways Stopes was conservative; she disapproved of abortion, masturbation, and lesbianism. On the other hand, she advocated many liberal positions. She had supported the suffragettes, she contended that "a married woman's body and soul should be essentially her own," and she urged Kipling to change the last line of "If" because it was unfair to women.

As the years went by, Stopes clinics appeared in Leeds, Aberdeen, Cardiff, Belfast, and elsewhere. The mobile van mentioned at the beginning of the chapter functioned for some months before it was burned down by Elizabeth Ellis, a Catholic who deemed it "a source of immorality and venereal disease." Stopes raised enough money to procure two more caravans.

In 1924, Stopes and Roe became the parents of a son, Henry (Harry) Stopes-Roe, a future scientist. Another child had been stillborn in 1919. Stopes became a very domineering mother, and when in time she opposed her son's choice of a wife, he defied her. This caused a rift between them, and there was never a complete reconciliation.

In the 1930s, Stopes and her husband became estranged. He had had serious financial losses, and he was less robust than when they had met. After World War I, he had no special niche in life but nevertheless objected to being known as the husband of Marie Stopes. During World War II, he served in the RAF (on the ground). By that time he was tolerated only occasionally as a visitor to the pretentious house bought by his wife. He died in 1949.

Dr. Helena Wright, a physician, noted in an interview that in 1928 Marie was showing signs of paranoia and megalomania. There are numerous examples to back up this view. Stopes's 1920 book entitled *A New Gospel to All Peoples* showed that she believed she was in touch with God. In 1921, when the coal miners threatened to strike, she offered her services to Lloyd George as a mediator. Some of her correspondence with the great and near-great suggests megalomania: for example, in 1940, she offered to join the War Cabinet. Turned down, she wrote to Churchill suggesting the air war be fought over Berlin.

As Stopes aged, she became increasingly difficult. Rigid in her ways, she had little interest in promoting research on improved contraceptive methods. Again in contrast to Margaret Sanger, she had scant interest in the dangers of the world's overpopulation.

Stopes's literary output was prodigious and for many years her royalties were considerable. Besides nonfiction, she wrote poetry and plays. She knew, entertained, and corresponded with personages such as George Bernard Shaw.

There is evidence that Stopes was not always thinking logically in her later years. She believed she would live until she was at least 120. She became romantically involved with a much younger Keith Briant, who later became her biographer, and with Baron Avro Manhattan, 35 years her junior.

Marie Stopes died of breast cancer on October 2, 1958, just before her seventy-eighth birthday.

Building upon Stopes's work, the British birth control movement has made great advances. The Lambeth Conference of Anglican Bishops in 1920 had officially opposed the idea of sexual union in marriage as an end in itself. After a period of ten years during which Stopes worked actively for birth control, the bishops gave approval to the use of artificial contraception. In 1958 the bishops stated that producing a family "is not the sole purpose of Christian marriage; implied within the bond of husband and wife is the relationship of love with its sacramental expression in physical union."

Stopes's Constructive Birth Control Society merged into the National Birth Control Council, which ultimately became the Family Planning Association.

By 1930, birth control information was permitted at maternal and child welfare centers—something long advocated by Stopes. She fought for birth control for married women, but by 1975 free contraceptive services were available to all British women, married or not.

The original Stopes clinic in Holloway relocated in 1925 to

Whitfield Street in central London. In accordance with Stopes's will, this clinic was later left to the Eugenics Society. Known as the Marie Stopes Memorial Clinic, from 1958 to 1976 it provided low-cost contraceptive services.

As the Family Planning Association's private clinics were turned over to the National Health Service, the future of the private Stopes Memorial Clinic was in jeopardy. In 1976, Population Services took over its management, with emphasis on meeting client (this was preferred to "patient") needs. For instance, clinic hours were set for the convenience of the clients rather than of the staff. Cervical smears (Pap tests) and breast examinations were part of "well-woman screening," an idea not then in vogue. The use of paramedical personnel was also promoted—something Stopes had heartily approved. Male and female fertilization are currently offered, and there are additional Marie Stopes Centres in various British cities and towns.

The Marie Stopes Annexe in Whitfield Street counsels women with unwanted pregnancies. In north London, the Marie Stopes Nursing Home now provides abortions on an outpatient or overnight basis. Stopes was strongly opposed to abortion, so the appropriateness of using her name in connection with the latter facility may be debatable. Although Stopes had written Pope Pius IX requesting his support, in 1930 his encyclical on marriage declared: "The conjugal act is of its very nature designed for the procreation of offspring. . . . Those, who, in performing it deliberately deprive it of its natural power and efficacy act against nature and do something which is shameful and intrinsically immoral." Stopes had made no dent in that quarter. In July 1959, the *London Times* noted that the Roman Catholic church did not condemn "natural methods of birth control"—complete abstinence or reliance on the so-called "safe period." Stopes's biographer Briant points out that to her this was the ultimate hypocrisy of the Catholic church.

When Stopes died, the *Times* reported, "Dr. Marie Stopes can fairly be said to have transformed the thought of her generation about the physical aspects of marriage and the role of contraception in married life."

Chapter 6

Mary Dennett

[By the end of another generation] people will more generally understand how to have babies *only* when they want them and can afford them. At present, unfortunately, it is against the law to give people [such] information.

—Mary Ware Dennett,
*The Sex Side of Life:
An Explanation for Young People,* 1918

Few women achieve the fame of Margaret Sanger or Marie Stopes; Mary Dennett, their contemporary, remained a lesser light in the birth control movement. Nevertheless, her conviction for using the mails to distribute an "obscene" pamphlet and her subsequent description of the trial gave unexpected and positive publicity to the birth control movement.

Mary Coffin Ware Dennett was born April 4, 1872, in Worcester, Massachusetts, to George Whitefield Ware and Livonia Coffin (Ames) Ware. She was the second of four children. George Ware was a wool merchant who seemed to have sufficient means to live comfortably. Both he and his wife were from New England families that Dennett termed "deathly respectable." When Dennett was ten, her father died and the family moved to Boston. Following graduation from high school, she entered a course of study in design at the Boston Museum of Fine Arts.

From 1894 to 1897, Dennett taught at Philadelphia's Drexel Institute, where she organized the School of Decorative Design. She was in her early twenties and had been asked by the administration not to reveal her age because of the possibility that her students would be considerably older than she was.

Study in Europe followed. Dennett's claim to fame in the world of arts and crafts is her rediscovery of the art of making Cordova leather wall hangings. This activity had been practiced in Spain and Italy during the Renaissance, but by the twentieth century, Dennett could find no craftsperson doing such work. Descriptions of how to prepare Cordoval leathers were first published in Venice in 1564. Translation had sometimes obscured clarity, and it was difficult to work out a process.

Dennett's sister Clara had also studied in the field, and together they started a handicraft shop in Boston, unique because the Ware women specialized in experimental leather gilding. By the end of three years, they gave a creditable exhibit of gilded leather.

In 1900 Mary married William Hartley Dennett, a Bostonian and an architect. The couple had three children, one of whom died in infancy. Dennett turned to home decorating, working with her husband. Her store became the Handicraft Shop of Boston, a cooperative venture that was successful both financially and artistically.

By 1910 Dennett and the boys were living in New York City without William, and three years later there was a divorce, apparently because William wanted it. The boys remained under the custody of their mother.

Dennett apparently had doubts about her creativity as an artist and believed that she should do what she could to make an atmosphere conducive to those with real talent.

Drawn to the issue of votes for women, Dennett had served as field secretary of the Massachusetts Woman Suffrage Association in the years 1908 to 1910. It was her position as corresponding secretary of the National American Woman Suffrage Association that brought her to New York. For the next four years, she was responsible for a campaign that brought suffragist pamphlets to all parts of the nation. Her leaflet entitled *The Real Point* remained popular for several years.

Close contact with the suffragist movement undoubtedly affected Dennett's future involvement with the birth control activists. Margaret Sanger took scant interest in the struggle to pass the 19th amendment; she also had little compunction about breaking the law. On the other hand, Carrie Chapman Catt, who dominated the suffagists, worked systematically to have the law changed, and her strategy was reflected in Dennett's attempts to overcome Comstockery.

Dennett had other reform interests besides the vote; she was attracted to the single-tax theory, socialism, and pacificism.

The single-tax theory, almost forgotten today, was developed by Henry George (1839–97). He contended that monetary progress was determined by the productive use of land and that owners who did no work were made rich by the toil of laborers. According to George, "From this fundamental injustice flow all the injustices which distort and endanger modern development, which condemn the producer of wealth to poverty and pamper the nonproducer in luxury, which rear the tenement house with the palace, plant the brothel behind the church, and compel us to build prisons as we open new schools." George's remedy was to require that all rents be paid to the government as the collective landlord; he contended that no other taxes would be necessary. Dennett's attraction to this and the other two philosophical theories underlines her interest in bettering the lot of others.

In 1916 Dennett became field secretary of the American Union against Militarism. She also worked actively to reelect President Wilson, although she herself was not yet entitled to vote. When the United States declared war on Germany on April 6, 1917, she resigned her position in the Women's Section of the Democratic National Committee. A short time later, she became a founder of a radical antiwar group called the People's Council. As Executive Secretary of the Hillquit Nonpartisan League, she supported Morris Hillquit, a Socialist candidate for mayor of New York.

As early as 1915, Dennett had been associated with the birth control movement, but her motivation is not clear. Some people of that era held that a burgeoning population induced war, and it has been suggested that Dennett's initial interest in birth control was related to pacifism.

Although Margaret Sanger always considered herself the founder of the National Birth Control League, others have disputed this. (Their claim is that in March 1915, Dennett plus Jessie Ashley and Clara Stillman organized the first national birth control association in the United States.) Late in 1914 Sanger had fled the country to avoid trial for breaking the law, and in her absence, Dennett and cohorts organized a campaign to have the Comstock laws changed. Who was the actual founder of the League is not clear.

The official declaration of principles adopted by the National Birth Control League was this:

> The object of the Birth Control League is to help in the formation of a body of public opinion that will result in the repeal of the laws, National, State or local, which make it a criminal offense, punishable by fine or imprisonment, or both, to print, publish or impart information regarding the control of human offspring by artificial methods of preventing conception.

Certainly Dennett would have been on familiar ground in such a group.

By 1918 a new organization named the Voluntary Parenthood League was formed, into which the National Birth Control League was absorbed. Education was important, but the focus was political.

At first there was concentration on changing state laws. Dennett's book, *Birth Control Laws*, published in 1924, explains the absurdity of some of these laws.

> They are very similar in import and phraseology to the parent Federal law, Section 211, but they deal with other ways of circulating contraceptive knowledge and means than transportation by mail or express. The 24 states which have specific prohibitions variously forbid publishing, advertising or giving information. Fourteen states prohibit any one to tell. (Fancy trying to enforce such a law!) In most of these States the statute is similar to that in the District of Columbia, which even forbids the *telling* of anything that "will be *calculated* to lead another" to apply any information to the prevention of conception, and also makes it a crime to have in one's possession any instructions to lend or give away.

Dennett worked hard to gain support from New York's legislators but did not succeed. When the state approach was considered ineffective, the women changed their tactics. According to Dennett herself: "In the summer of 1919, as Director of the Voluntary Parenthood League, I went to Washington, to begin a quiet survey of Congress with a view to obtaining a sponsor for the bill which was the aim of the League — namely to 'remove the words *preventing conception* from the federal obscenity laws.'"

The preliminary work continued for two and a half years. From recorded information, it was clear that most members of the Senate practiced family limitation. In her book entitled *Who's Obscene?* Dennett describes her struggle with the Senate:

> Like most sophisticated Americans, the members evidently had obtained information on the subject, regardless of law or legal "decency"; and quite as obviously, in view of the existence of their families, the majority of them were neither sterile nor ascetic. Yet member after member decided it would be better were someone else to introduce the bill by which *all citizens* might have legal and decent access to the forbidden knowledge. Fourteen Senators, all of whom believed in the bill, declined to introduce it, and one who had promised — in writing — to sponsor the bill, proved faithless to his word.

There was some reason to hope that a case could be made for the restoration of constitutional freedom of communication. With this in mind, Dennett interviewed Dr. Hubert Work, then assistant postmaster general. Excerpts from her notes show the kind of situation she was sometimes combatting:

> I began by saying, "I assume your recognition of the merit of controlled parenthood as distinguished from haphazard parenthood." He said no, that he had fixed ideas which could be stated in one sentence, namely, "sterilize all boys and girls who are unfit to become parents and then let nature take its course unhindered." I reminded him that his individual opinion was exceptional for these days, but that it might not prevent his seeing that Section 211 of the Penal Code needed reconstruction, that it contained three unrelated matters, all lumped under obscenity — viz: pornographic literature, abortion and the control of conception.

Dennett got nowhere with Dr. Work. Her notes end: "Said he was glad I had come, because of the two doctors who had sent me, and 'because of your own personality.' To which latter remark I showed resentment, reminding him that my errand was on behalf of millions of suffering people, and was not personal."

In her book, Dennett also describes an encounter with Horace J. Donnelly, assistant solicitor:

> He introduced the subject of the suppression of Marie Stopes's book, *Married Love*, and inquired with an undisguised salacious smile if I knew the book and liked it and thought it ought to be circulated. His manner was decidedly repulsive, but his expression sombered perceptibly when I answered that I wished every married man in the United States were obliged to read the book—that it would educate them in ways in which many of them were sadly deficient—that life would be considerably cleaner, sweeter, more decent and lovely if people were brought up in harmony with Dr. Stopes's ideals. This remark seemed to stir his own sense of decency into activity, and the conversation was considerably more productive after that.

The Voluntary Parenthood League published *The Birth Control Herald*, which Dennett edited. The first issue stated: "Possibly Dr. Work might welcome a practical suggestion, namely, that he promptly request Congress to change this futile law which has encumbered the statute books since Anthony Comstock got it passed in 1873. Any law that can't be generally enforced should be repealed." The last sentence was one of Dennett's sincere beliefs and an argument that she used frequently. In 1990, Harvard's legal authority Laurence Tribe expressed the same sentiment: "No rational society makes laws it cannot hope to enforce."

Senator Albert A. Cummins of Iowa, who at long last had agreed to be cosponsor of the bill to change the law, said later that it was difficult to get men to consider the subject seriously because "it still seemed a joke."

Ridiculed and insulted, Dennett labored assiduously on behalf of the bill until 1925. At that time, she resigned from the Voluntary Parenthood League. It had become clear to her that the proposed legislation was not about to pass; to add to her stress, she was at odds with fellow-members in the League about physician control in making contraception available.

As we have seen, Margaret Sanger finally made concessions to the medical profession. Dennett, in contrast, firmly believed that all legal restraints should be removed from the dissemination of contraceptive information and therefore considered the authority of the medical profession a restraint. She rejected "a legalized monopoly of knowledge"; to her it was an issue of fairness. "Fancy real live Americans wanting freedom for doctors only," she wrote to a friend, "and being willing to let the laws provide that anyone who passes along what the doctor tells, is guilty of obscenity." For Dennett it was the last straw when the Voluntary Parenthood League adopted the Sanger position, voting to support the "doctors only" position.

The relationship between Sanger and Dennett had never been good. As we have seen, the Voluntary Parenthood League supported the former when she was on trial for organizing a birth control clinic. In 1916 Dennett had asked Sanger to serve on the executive board of the National Birth Control League, and she had repeated that offer in 1919 for the Voluntary Parenthood League, but Sanger refused.

Dennett agreed to write for *The Birth Control Review* and become a member of its board. The magazine's editorial policy adopted in 1919 dictated that the content should deal with birth control and omit all propaganda. When Sanger disregarded this policy, urging all women to join in a strike to protest the unlimited reproduction of poorly paid workers, Dennett resigned. Sanger claimed that denying birth control to such women workers was a form of exploitation. Dennett considered Sanger's stand too militant, and the League from the beginning was against that approach. Dennett had further objections to terms and tactics that related the birth control movement to the labor movement.

Although a letter exists in which Sanger expressed her dislike for Dennett, the Sanger *Autobiography* gave this appraisal of Dennett:

> Mrs. Dennett was a good promoter and experienced campaigner, a capable office executive, an indefatigable worker for suffrage and peace, with a background that might have been invaluable. I often regretted that we could not have combined our efforts.

Sanger's critics have suggested that some of the material in her autobiography is aimed at making readers think what the author wants them to think. This judgment of Dennett could well fit into that category, since it makes Sanger appear more generous than she actually was. In any case, the two women did seem incapable of working together effectively, although both were dedicated and gifted. In contrast to Sanger, however, Dennett was reserved; she also lacked Sanger's flamboyancy and some of her vision.

As noted, Dennett and Marie Stopes had met during a visit by the latter to New York. Correspondence between the pair makes it clear that Stopes's approach to reform in reproductive rights was more appealing to Dennett than was Sanger's. The published works of the three women also indicate that Dennett's objectives were closer to Stopes's than to Sanger's.

Dennett's resignation from the Voluntary Parenthood League did not end her effort to fight the Comstock laws. Her 1926 book, *Birth Control Laws*, was a thorough analysis of the statutes and a logical presentation of reasons for their repeal.

In 1928 Dennett was indicted for mailing an "obscene" pamphlet, *The Sex Side of Life*, of which she was the author. Dennett originally wrote the controversial pamphlet for her sons, then 11 and 14. It was published in 1918 in *The Medical Review of Reviews*. About a year later, she put it out herself, charging 25 cents for a single copy and less when quantities were ordered. About 25,000 copies were so distributed to church organizations, health departments, and other groups, all of whom had requested it.

In 1922, the postmaster general banned the mailing of *The Sex Side of Life*.

IT IS A CRIMINAL OFFENSE

To send or Recive [sic] Obscene or Indecent Matter by Mail or Express

The forbidden matter includes anything printed or written, or any indecent pictures, or any directions, drugs or articles for the prevention of conception, etc.

The offense is punishable by a *Five Thousand Dollar Fine, or Five Years in the Penitentiary or Both.*

Ignorance of the law is no excuse.

> For more detailed information on this subject read Sections 480
> and 1078 of the Postal Laws and Regulations, which may be con-
> sulted at any post office.

Not intimidated by his action, Dennett continued to send out the
pamphlet first class. By 1928 the Post Office had indicted the
work as "lewd, lascivious, filthy, vile and indecent." (A decoy address was used to obtain evidence.) Dennett's opponents found
particularly offensive her statement signifying that the act of sex
can bring great pleasure, that medical science might find a cure
for venereal disease, and that masturbation is harmless and not a
cause of insanity. Dennett's pamphlet includes, for example,
these passages:

> When a man and woman fall in love so that they really belong to
> each other, the physical side of the relation is this: both of them feel
> at intervals a peculiar thrill or glow, particularly in the sexual
> organs, and it naturally culminates after they have gone to bed at
> night. The man's special sex organ or penis, becomes enlarged and
> stiffened, instead of soft and limp as ordinarily, and thus it easily
> enters the passage into the woman's body called the vagina or birth-
> canal, which leads to the uterus or womb. . . . The penis and vagina
> are about the same size, as Nature intended them to fit each other.
> By a rhythmic movement of the penis in and out, the sex act
> reaches an exciting climax or orgasm, when there is for the woman
> a particularly satisfying contracture of the muscles of the passage
> and for the man, the expulsion of the semen, the liquid which con-
> tains the germs of life. This is followed by a sensation of peaceful
> happiness and sleepy relaxation. It is the very greatest physical
> pleasure to be had in all human experience. . . .

> Many prostitutes become diseased, and there is, as yet, no way for
> either them or the men who visit them to be positively safe from in-
> fection. But the doctors are making progress in their study of these
> diseases, and they are finding out how to control or cure them, just
> as they have in the case of tuberculosis. . . .

> Boys and girls sometimes get the habit of handling their sex organs
> so as to get them excited. This is called masturbation or self-abuse.
> It is also called auto-erotism. Such handling cam be made to result
> in a climax something like that of the natural sex act. For genera-
> tions this habit has been considered wrong and dangerous but
> recently many of the best scientists have concluded that the chief
> harm has come from the worry caused by doing it, when one believed
> it to be wrong.

The judge requested statements from experts on behalf of both the prosecution and the defense. Many authorities supplied testimony on Dennett's behalf.

Rabbit Stephen Wise of the Free Synagogue in New York City wrote:

> I should be entirely willing to put it in the hand of an adolescent child or grandchild of my own. I wish that children might learn about the sex side of life from a source as clean and wholesome as this is, as compared with what are, alas, the much less clean and unwholesome sources from which most children derive their sex information. I cannot find anything obscene therein.

According to Dr. Katherine B. Davis, head of the New York's Bureau of Social Hygiene: "The pamphlet is simple, direct, explicit, with scientifically precise names... If this is 'obscene,' then what *are* elders to give young people when they demand facts? It will be a great pity if parents and teachers are deprived of this means of solving a difficult problem."

Dr. Robert L. Dickinson, noted obstetrician and gynecologist, responded: "The Dennett pamphlet, as a statement of facts, is substantially correct. As a method of presentation, it is desirable and most timely. Its brevity and simplicity commend it."

Experts also submitted opinions on behalf of the prosecution in this 1929 trial.

The Rev. John Roach Straton, pastor of the Calvary Baptist Church in New York, declared:

> I feel that *the book is a positive and deadly menace* and not only ought to be suppressed but those connected with its preparation and circulation, outside of the medical and scientific fields, ought to be punished to the full extent of the law, as a rebuke to such teaching and as an example to all people that America will no longer tolerate tampering with the very foundations of a pure, healthy and happy social system.

Dr. Howard Kelly, eminent professor emeritus of gynecology at Johns Hopkins University, had this to say: "I am astounded that anyone should have dared to bring so obscene a piece of literature to an eighth printing in a land which has any laws at all to protect its young manhood and womanhood from unutterable defilement, and that its author has so far escaped incarceration."

George B. Murphy, chaplain of St. John's Long Island City Hospital, opposed *The Sex Side of Life* for a number of reasons, among them his beliefs that the pamphlet condoned free love and preached birth control.

The case was tried in Brooklyn. Defending Dennett was Morris Ernst, later known to Sanger followers for the famous "One Package" decision. He gave his services gratis. A newspaper article about the Dennett affair described Mary as a slight and benign figure, noting her carefully waved white hair.

Despite much glowing testimony, Dennett was declared guilty and fined $300. Ernst at once appealed, and Dennett declared:

> I shall not pay any fine, no matter how small, either now or later, nor shall I allow anyone to do it for me.
>
> If the few government officials who are responsible for this prosecution wish to use the power which the law gives them to penalize me for the work I have done on behalf of the young people of the country, then they must stand the shame of making it a prison sentence, not a fine.

SENTENCES OF BIRTH CONTROL ADVOCATES

FEDERAL

Margaret Sanger, New York .... 1914 Federal case— dismissed, 9 indictments.
Mrs. Rhea C. Kachel, Philadelphia, Pa. .... 25.00 fine
Mr. Fred Merkel, Reading, Pa. .... 25.00 fine
William Sanger, New York .... 30 days—workhouse
Emma Goldman, New York .... 15 days
Joseph Macario, San Francisco .... Freed
Emma Goldman, Portland, Ore. .... Freed
Dr. Ben L. Reitman, Portland, Ore. .... Freed
Margaret Sanger, Portland, Ore. .... Freed
Carl Rave, Portland, Ore. .... $10.00 fine

Herbert Smith, Seattle, Wash. .... 25.00 fine
Van Kleeck Allison, Boston, Mass. .... 60 days
Steven Kerr, New York .... 15 days
Peter Marner, New York .... 15 days
Bolton Hall, New York .... Freed
Jessie Ashley, New York .... $100.00 fine
Emma Goldman, New York .... Freed
Dr. Ben L. Reitman, New York .... 60 days
Ethel Byrne, New York .... 30 days
            (Pardoned during hunger strike.)
Dr. Ben L. Reitman, Cleveland, O. .... 6 mos.
            ($1000 fine and costs.)
Margaret Sanger, New York .... 30 days
Kitty Marion, New York .... 30 days—workhouse

From *Birth Control Laws*, by Mary Ware Dennett.

The trial engendered publicity for Dennett and her cause. The *New York Daily News* noted that there existed at least one book where young people could learn the facts of life "without hysteria or dirt or bunk." The *Detroit Free Press* termed the conviction a medieval verdict. The *New York Herald Tribune* stated: "[The defendant] can justly claim that hers is a test case of national moment, and the fact that it is so is largely due to the dignity and clear-mindedness with which Mrs. Dennett has herself regarded the whole matter."

Throughout the United States, there was sympathy for Dennett and for what she stood. Many civic and social organizations passed resolutions of protest at the verdict. With the aid of the American Civil Liberties Union, a National Defense Committee was formed, its goal to appeal the case to the Supreme Court. That did not prove necessary. In 1930 the Second Circuit Court of Appeals in New York, through an opinion by Judge Augustus N. Hand, ruled that the Comstock laws (in New York State) should not interfere with serious, scientific sex instruction unless such information is "clearly indecent."

Dennett's *Who's Obscene?* (published in 1930) is a detailed discussion about the trial. She was sufficiently interested in the subject of children's sex education to write a book about it in 1931.

Mary Ware Dennett, 1930
Courtesy of the Schlesinger Library, Radcliffe College.

It is interesting to note that the book that meant the most to Dennett was Havelock Ellis's *The Dance of Life* (1923).

For many years, Dennett lived in Astoria, Long Island. Pacifism was never far from her mind. From 1941 to 1944, she served as first chairperson of the World Federalists, an organization whose goal was to gain peace through world government and international law.

Dennett died in a nursing home in Valatie, New York, in 1947. An unexpected and unusual tribute came from her old rival, Margaret Sanger. In a letter to Havelock Ellis about Dennett's trial, America's leader of the birth control movement wrote: "It's outrageous that she should be convicted.... She has more nerve in her old age than she had when she was in the B.C. fight.... It's encouraging that people do change—and for the better."

Chapter 7

Mary Calderone

> We try to describe rather than advocate, to explain all
> sides of a subject on which serious professionals in the
> field might disagree.
> —Mary Calderone and Eric Johnson,
> *The Family Book About Sexuality,*
> Rev. ed., 1989

Mary Calderone's fame is in the field of human sexuality,
particularly as it pertains to adolescents. Her professional training
as a physician gave authority to what she said and wrote about
masturbation and other subjects, and especially about birth control and abortion.

Calderone was born on July 1, 1904, in New York City to Edward and Clara (Smith) Steichen, the first of two daughters.
Edward Steichen was a noted photographer. He claimed that
Calderone possessed leadership ability at an early age, but her
strong personality caused no conflict between them. In fact, she
considered among the chief influences on her life and career her
"extraordinary father's extension of photography into the area of
human life and the human condition."

After study in France and New York, Calderone entered
Vassar College, where she majored in chemistry and graduated in
1925. During her college years, she participated in dramatics, an
interest she pursued by studying for three years under Richard
Boleslavsky and Marie Ouspenskaya of the American Laboratory
Theater. But Calderone was ambitious. She knew she could not

compete with Katharine Cornell—who shared the rank of first lady of the American stage with Lynn Fontaine and Helen Hayes—and so decided to drop acting.

In 1926 Calderone had married an actor named Lon Martin. They had two daughters, the older of whom died of pneumonia at age eight. The marriage ended in divorce in 1933. With many important plans shattered, Calderone sought help in psychoanalysis.

Test results showed that Calderone was strong in science. This prompted her to consider medicine as a career, and in 1933 she entered the medical school of the University of Rochester. Having obtained an M.D. four years later, she did an internship in pediatrics at New York City's Bellevue Hospital. Then with the aid of a fellowship from the city's Department of Public Health, she obtained a master's degree in public health from Columbia University in 1942.

This move affected Calderone's life not only professionally but personally. The district health officer of the Lower East Side was Dr. Frank Calderone, the son of Italian immigrants, and Calderone worked under him. He would soon move on to become the city's deputy chief commissioner of health, and he later became chief administrative officer of the World Health Organization and director of health services with the United Nations Secretariat. When he died in 1987, he was considered an authority on preventive medicine. The couple were married in 1941, and Mary Calderone herself remained in public health.

Following several years as physician for the school system of Great Neck, Long Island, Mary Calderone was appointed medical director of Margaret Sanger's organization, Planned Parenthood Federation of America, in 1953. She would hold this position for almost 11 years.

"The gift of sex generally is something the American culture has abnegated," Calderone said in a 1961 lecture, noting that conflicting religious philosophies were often responsible for this abnegation. Her aim was the acceptance of birth control as a public health venture, and she worked tirelessly towards that goal. Her numerous lectures were directed to both lay and professional audiences. She also made radio and TV appearances. According

Mary Steichen Calderone ca. 1927
Courtesy of the Schlesinger Library, Radcliffe College.

to *Current Biography*, it was largely because of her influence that the American Medical Association in 1964 adopted its policy permitting physicians to dispense birth control information as a matter of course. (Twenty-seven years had passed since the organization gave its approval to contraception.) Calderone was the editor of *Family Planning and Contraceptive Practice* (1964; revised edition, 1970), the first comprehensive medical textbook in the area.

In 1958, Planned Parenthood sponsored a conference on abortion; Calderone was part of the steering committee. Present were specialists in obstetrics, psychology, public health, biology, sociology, forensic medicine, the law, and demography. The papers presented were later edited by Calderone and published in 1958 under the title *Abortion in the United States*. This conference, of course, predated the 1973 Supreme Court decision that legalized abortion. Some of the statements recorded in the conference proceedings are interesting in the light of what has since developed:

> "We should take the stand, in a democratic way, that no religious group should seek to maintain the religious and ethical standards of its own members by the imposition of laws applied to the general population." — Dr. Theodore Lidz, professor of psychiatry, Yale University School of Medicine

> "But is it not true that fundamentally most therapeutic abortions are actually being granted because of socioeconomic and humanitarian reasons that are masked as psychiatric or humanitarian reasons? ... I would like to suggest that ... this conference is faced with the direct challenge of formulating ways in which the law can be changed." — Dr. Mary Calderone

The Conference participants recognized that present laws and mores have not served to control the practice of illegal abortion. Rather, this has continued to an extent ignored, or perhaps, condoned by a large proportion of the general public and even of the medical and legal professions. To keep on the books, unchallenged, laws that do not receive public sanction and observance is of questionable service to our society. Indeed, the demonstrated high incidence of terminations of unwanted pregnancies by illegal abortion could be looked upon as a disease of that society, presenting a problem in epidemiology as real and as urgent as did venereal disease three decades ago. There is a great similarity between the two, since both involve health, mores, and morals. Until comparatively recently the physicians and the public health agencies of America were constrained from facing the venereal disease problem openly without prejudice or prudery. As soon as they did, it became possible to apply medical and public health controls, and a majority of those attending the Conference felt that the same type of frontal assault should now be made on the problem of intentional abortion. It was recognized by Conference participants that although the effort to obtain an induced abortion may indicate that the woman is physically ill, more often it reflects one or more of a complexity of factors such as: poor social or economic environment, disturbed marital relations, psychiatric or neurotic disturbance within the family, or, quite simply, a need to keep her family at its present size. Abortion, whether legal or illegal, is a traumatic experience and in many instances its commission does not solve the basic problem. . . . The goal should be to reduce [the number of abortions] as far as possible, but it is apparent that this reduction cannot be effected within the framework of present attitudes and laws. The abortion problem must therefore become the candid concern of physicians, sociologists, educators, religious leaders, lawyers, legislators, demographers, and other responsible citizens. It is only by the most courageous and honest action of these groups working together that this urgent problem can be solved. — Summary statement

Although always an advocate of the cause of birth control, Calderone's interest was drawn more and more to studying human sexuality. In 1961 the National Council of Churches sponsored the first North American Conference on Church and Family for sociologists, religious leaders, family life educators, public health officials, and others. Five hundred delegates from twenty-eight Protestant denominations gathered to discuss psychological problems in the light of Christian faith and practice. Calderone, a staunch Quaker, was one of the twelve resource persons asked to speak. Later she joined five colleagues from the conference to form an informal committee to look into studies concerned with human sexuality. The ultimate outcome of this was SIECUS, the Sex Information and Education Council of the United States, founded in 1964.

During her tenure with Planned Parenthood, Calderone was impressed with the large volume of mail requesting information not only on contraception, but also on all manner of sexual problems. "They were desperate for information on how to teach children about sexual behavior, how to handle out-of-wedlock pregnancies. . . . Handing out contraceptives was not enough," she told an interviewer. She left Planned Parenthood to become executive director of SIECUS, located in New York City.

When Calderone resigned from Planned Parenthood, she was almost 60; she was a grandmother, but her youngest daughter was still in high school. The family hobby was sailing, and their schooner *Tradition* had covered hundreds of miles from Nova Scotia to the West Indies. Calderone's own avocations were cooking and growing house plants.

The stated purpose of SIECUS was expressed in these terms:

> To establish man's sexuality as a health entity; to identify the special characteristics that distinguish it from, yet relate it to, human reproduction; to dignify it by openness of approach, study, and scientific research designed towards its understanding and its freedom from exploitation; to give leadership to professionals and to society, to the end that human beings may be aided towards responsible use of the sexual faculty and towards assimilation of sex into their individual life patterns as a creative and re-creative force.

SIECUS issued the following position statement on masturbation:

> Sexual self-pleasing, or masturbation, is a natural part of sexual behavior for individuals of all ages. It can help to develop a sense of the body as belonging to the self and an affirmative attitude toward the body as a legitimate source of enjoyment. It can also help in the release of tension in a way harmless to the self and to others, and provide an intense experience of the self in preparation for experiencing another. Masturbation and the fantasies that frequently accompany it, can be a subtle way of maintaining or restoring the image of one's self as a fully functioning human being.

During the first year of SIECUS's existence, Calderone traveled thousands of miles to address high school and college students, parents, and professionals such as educators and religious leaders. A dynamic speaker, she was noted for her candor, and her talks were very popular.

Calderone believed that in general parents are the best sex educators. She thought that parents should begin giving information in a positive manner at the kindergarten level and continue through adolescence. "Parents give a child his basic sex education through what they project as to their feelings about themselves, how they treat each other, how they treat the child. Parents must accept their own sexuality, then they must accept a child's sexuality," Calderone said in an interview in 1974. She contended that although accurate biological information is essential, it does not constitute good sex education; young people must understand all types of human relationships and consider sex within that context. They must also have opportunity to discuss these matters, preferably with parents and peers. And Calderone emphasized the importance of responsibility in sexual relationships.

It is not uncommon for parents to refuse to take any part in educating their children about sex, and for this reason, educators looked to SIECUS for help with integrating sex into the K–12 curriculum. Groups opposed to sex education in the schools objected, for example, to telling youngsters that sex is pleasurable. As antagonism grew, the new organization was accused of leaning towards communism. (In that era this was a common accusation leveled against groups suggesting almost anything unconventional.) Calderone, as the leader of SIECUS, was the target of a vicious hate campaign. Critics had this complaint, still heard today: sex education whets the child's curiosity and may lead to sexual experimentation at a much earlier age than would otherwise occur.

Calderone's answer was that children inevitably learn about sex and that they should have accurate information, rather than information acquired by chance. She noted that her faith sustained her when "terrible things were said." Admitting that she was willing to say things people were scared to say, she stated: "But I don't see myself as at all courageous. I was simply in a good position to do this and someone had to."

Calderone has been a successful author. As Mary Steichen Martin, she wrote with her father *The First Picture Book: Everyday Things for Babies* (1930) and *The Second Picture Book* (1931). Her medically oriented publications have been well received. Following the book on abortion, she edited *Release from Sexual Tensions* (1960), *Manual of Family Planning and Contraceptive Practice* (1964; revised edition, 1971), and *Sexuality and Human Values* (1974). With Eric W. Johnson as coauthor, she wrote *The Family Book About Sexuality* (1981; revised edition, 1989).

Calderone made this statement for *Contemporary Authors*:

> My motivation for writing is simple: to give ordinary people access to the facts scientists now have about different aspects of human

sexuality common to all people everywhere, as well as of the varia-
tions that occur as the result of socialization patterns that are
specific to different societies and cultures. Such knowledge, when
understood, accepted, and applied at appropriate times between
birth and death, can undoubtedly serve in positive rather than the
negative ways we now see. It can act to avoid or prevent many of
the sexual dysfunctions easily observable in our society and elsewhere. It is this stance of mine [taken more than two decades ago],
and persistently developed and maintained, that has slowly but
surely enlisted the support and active participation of the scientific
world today in many parts of the globe.

In the opinion of the author, *The Family Book About Sexuality*
is exceptional for several reasons: the level of the writing is suitable for two generations, subjects such as homosexuality are dealt
with in a sensitive manner, and controversial issues such as abortion are given even-handed treatment so that readers can make informed decisions. (Calderone is on record in favor of protecting
abortion rights.)

In 1982 the board of directors at SIECUS announced that
after 18 years of service to that organization as cofounder, executive director, and president, Dr. Mary Steichen Calderone
had resigned. Her new position would be adjunct professor at
New York University, where she would be associated with the
human sexuality program in the health education department.
She was almost 78.

Calderone has received numerous honors and honorary
degrees. Two in particular demonstrate the effectiveness of her
work. The *Ladies' Home Journal* in 1971 named her one of
America's 75 most important women. Four years later, the
Newspaper Enterprises Association cited her as one of the 50
most influential women in the United States. Also, it is to
Calderone's credit that in 1985 a Louis Harris poll showed that
85 percent of parents in the United States agreed that sexuality
education should be taught in public schools.

There was another indication that sexuality was being
discussed openly: Dr. Ruth became almost a household word,
thanks first to radio and later to television programs by sex
therapist Dr. Ruth Westheimer.

Edward Steichen used to tell his daughter that with the right outlook, you do not ever have to grow old. She seems to have taken his advice—when the 1989 edition of *The Family Book* was published, its senior author was 85.

Perhaps a remark made to the press by Frank Calderone best sums up his wife's abilities: "She's damn good at everything."

Chapter 8

Katharine McCormick

You must, indeed, feel a certain pride in your judgment.
Gregory Pincus had been working for at least ten years on
the progesterone of reproductive processes in animals. He
had practically no money for this work.... Then you
came along with your fine interest and enthusiasm and
with your faith and ... things began to happen.
—Letter from Margaret Sanger to
Katharine McCormick, 1956

Katharine Dexter McCormick was a philanthropist with a
sharp intellectual curiosity. Her financial contribution to research
that resulted in the development of a contraceptive pill gives her
a unique position in the birth control movement.

McCormick was born in Dexter, Michigan, on August 27,
1875, to Wirt and Josephine (Moore) Dexter; she was the second
of two children. Her father was a prominent lawyer with roots going
back to New England. Her mother was also a New Englander
and had taught school in Springfield, Massachusetts. Brought up
in affluence, Katharine developed into a beautiful and intelligent
young woman. After her husband's death in 1889 and that of her
son five years later, Josephine Dexter moved to Boston, where her
daughter accompanied her.

Katharine McCormick wanted more than the money and
social prestige that she already commanded; in particular, she
desired the rigorous education provided by the Massachusetts Institute
of Technology. For a woman to acquire such an education
was indeed a challenge, but one McCormick welcomed. She even

approved of MIT's policy of "permitting the survival of only the fittest of its students." Obviously it was important to be well prepared, so this determined young woman studied for three years as a special student at MIT before seeking regular admission, which she achieved in 1900. In 1904, at the age of 29, McCormick received the bachelor of science degree in biology, the second woman to graduate from MIT. The title of her senior thesis was "Fatigue of the Cardiac Muscle in Reptilia." With this scientific background, she could appreciate the complexity of trying to regulate reproduction through hormonal manipulation.

Stanley McCormick, the youngest son of Cyrus McCormick, courted Katharine during her college days. (Cyrus McCormick had invented the mechanical reaper and founded what was to become the International Harvester Company.) The couple were married in 1904 at the Dexter château on Lake Geneva in Switzerland. Stanley was an heir to great wealth and also a man of ability and promise. The bride and groom had several interests in common. Both enjoyed outdoor sports—tennis in particular. Art lovers, they acquired works of Monet and Manet, and they also shared an appreciation of music.

But tragedy intervened. Very soon Stanley was showing symptoms of serious mental disease. In 1906 he had to resign from International Harvester; by 1909 he had been declared legally incompetent. His condition did not improve, and for 40 years he received what would be considered custodial care (with every amenity that money could buy) at a McCormick estate in Santa Barbara, California. He died when he was 73.

Katharine McCormick's life was, of course, dramatically affected by her husband's illness. She spent considerable time at her husband's estate and also traveled abroad with her mother, becoming fluent in French and Italian. As time passed, however, McCormick seems to have become a recluse and was termed eccentric.

At the same time, McCormick worked hard for her favorite causes, one of which was woman suffrage. Through this movement, which she joined in 1909, she became acquainted with Mary Dennett. These two, together with other women, organized almost a hundred outdoor rallies and also lobbied at the Massachusetts state legislature. McCormick served as treasurer as well as vice president of the National American Woman Suffrage Association, the organization led by Carrie Chapman Catt. When its publication, the *Woman's Journal,* was short of funds, she contributed $6000 to cover the deficit. Through the International Suffrage Alliance, McCormick met Dr. Aletta Jacobs, the birth control pioneer from the Netherlands. The imposing château that had been the site of the Dexter-McCormick wedding was sometimes used for suffrage meetings. With Carrie Catt, McCormick was a founder of the League of Women Voters and served under Catt as its first vice president.

The first meeting between Margaret Sanger and McCormick took place in 1917. When Sanger's Clinical Research Bureau was having difficulty in the 1920s to obtain sufficient diaphragms, McCormick was among those who smuggled them into New York from Europe. When Sanger arranged a grand reception for the 300 delegates attending the 1927 World Population Conference, McCormick loaned the château for the occasion. Their correspondence, which continued for decades, shows that McCormick had a deep interest in contraceptive research. Sanger, of course, knew the importance of a continuing search for improved methods. She was particularly keen on a method independent of coitus that would be under female control, and McCormick had similar sentiments. In his excellent history of the birth control movement, James Reed expresses the opinion that McCormick, knowing that a devastating illness such as Stanley had might be inherited, was impressed with the importance of reliable birth control methodology.

McCormick had control of some Dexter funds, and after a lawsuit, she eventually controlled a large amount of McCormick money. Although much of it was not readily available to her until after Stanley's death, she gave what she could to her particular interests. This included substantial support for research on birth control, with the projects made known to her by Sanger. McCormick's largess was distinguished by one characteristic: she made it her business to know exactly how the money was being spent, and her intellect, curiosity, and scientific training made this possible. Her lawyer later declared: "She welcomed advice, listened to the opinion of others, spent endless hours going over every aspect of the problem to make sure that the ultimate result, regardless of time and expense, would measure up to her conception of what would be a fitting memorial to Stanley."

McCormick had of course sought help for her husband from authorities in psychiatry. When psychoanalysis failed to improve him, she turned to endocrinology. In 1927 she set up the Neuroendocrine Research Foundation to support a basic research project at Harvard Medical School. The scientist in charge, Roy G. Hoskins, was looking into the possibility that a deficiency of the adrenal gland was responsible for the symptoms of schizophrenia, the disease Stanley was thought to have. Because of his illness, his wife was at liberty to spend large sums on the foundation. By the 1930s, some schizophrenic patients at Worcester (Massachusetts) State Hospital had been treated with hormones from the adrenal cortex, but without improvement. The Neuroendocrine Research Foundation closed in 1947, when McCormick's support ceased.

A few years later McCormick began to support the research of Gregory Goodwin Pincus. Pincus was born in 1903, the son of Russian Jews who had immigrated to the United States. His graduate training at Harvard was in genetics. After postgraduate study in England and Germany, he returned to his alma mater in 1930 to work in the department of general physiology, concentrating his research on fertilization and ovum growth in rabbits.

In common with many promising young scientists, Pincus did not have tenure at Harvard. He was embittered by that institution's decision to terminate his employment after the academic year 1937-38, which he was spending at Cambridge University. There has been speculation about why Pincus was not given tenure; whatever the reasons, as a married man with a family, he obviously had to find something else soon.

Hudson Hoagland, a former colleague of Pincus at Harvard, was at the time in charge of the biology department at Clark University in Worcester. He offered his friend a position at Clark as visiting professor; the post was without salary but would provide some facilities for research. Baron Nathaniel Rothschild, a member of the British peerage and another investigator in the field of reproduction, knew Pincus at Cambridge University, and he came forward with a salary for two years. Hoagland induced a New York businessman to contribute moving expenses to enable the Pincus family to return to the States. The Josiah Macy, Jr., Foundation granted research funds. These financial arrangements were necessary because the Depression was still lingering and the postwar era of government-supported research had not yet arrived.

Pincus, along with more than a dozen other scientists whom Hoagland had recruited, existed in this hand-to-mouth environment until 1944. The group focused its efforts on the role of steroids in selected biological processes.

A steroid contains a complex chemical structure that is part of cholesterol and certain hormones—the estrogens and progesterone, for example. Hormones are blood-borne messengers that regulate cell function. Estrogens play an important part in the ovarian cycle; they are necessary for the development of secondary sex characteristics in females. Progesterone, sometimes called progestin, prepares the lining of the uterus for implantation of an ovum; it is essential for the maintenance of pregnancy.

In 1944, Hoagland and Pincus founded the Worcester Foundation for Experimental Biology, which provided an opportunity for bright scientists to work without the constraints of the academic world. Their institution prospered, thanks in part to Hoagland's skill in fund-raising. (His scientific expertise was in the field of brain chemistry.)

Drug companies were beginning to show great interest in the use of hormones for medical treatment. It was inevitable that Pincus's experience with the action of hormones in reproduction would become valuable to their endeavor. The G. D. Searle Company consulted him about producing inexpensive cortisone, a hormone effective in the treatment of rheumatoid arthritis, among other conditions. Pincus recommended a procedure that used bovine adrenals to manufacture cortisone. The process worked but was costly. An investigator from a competitor, Upjohn, soon perfected a process whereby microorganisms carried out the reactions, making an acceptable and far cheaper product.

Searle took a huge financial loss and that company's esteem of Pincus fell.

By 1951 Pincus was investigating steroids as contraceptives under a small grant from the Planned Parenthood Federation of America. As far back as 1937, other workers had shown that in rats large injections of progesterone inhibited ovulation, the release of a newly ripened egg from the ovary. Pincus confirmed this and obtained similar results when he used rabbits. Moreover, a dose given orally seemed to be effective. Because of its convenience, an oral contraceptive would be particularly attractive. (It is now believed that in antiquity and later periods, certain substances given by mouth were effective in preventing pregnancy.) Spearheading this work on oral contraceptives was a brilliant Chinese scientist named Min-Chueh Chang. Chang had obtained a Ph.D. from Cambridge University, and Pincus had recruited him to Shrewsbury from Strangeways Laboratory at Cambridge. (The Worcester Foundation is located in Shrewsbury, near Worcester.)

In a progress report to Planned Parenthood, Pincus stated: "These data demonstrate definitely the contraceptive-ovulation-inhibiting activity of an oral progestin, and suggest that with proper dosage and regimen of administration control of ovulation may be effective."

When McCormick visited Pincus in 1951, she told him of her hope that a relatively simple and foolproof method of oral contraception might be developed through laboratory research. Around the same time, Pincus began to appreciate the seriousness of the so-called population explosion. The scientist was now stimulated to act, but there remained the problem of obtaining the funds to make a thorough investigation of the suppression of ovulation.

Contraception was still a controversial issue. As Pincus himself explained in 1965: "Birth control and the allied areas of sexual physiology and sexual behavior have long been battlegrounds of opinion-voicers. They have suffered from clashes among differing culture patterns, theologies, moralities, even politics."

McCormick, now 77, had sold her dead husband's estate in

Santa Barbara and had settled in Boston, which was close to Shrewsbury. At last her finances were in order. Sanger made sure that McCormick had up-to-date details of Pincus's work with progesterone. Planned Parenthood and Searle, the latter no longer overly enthusiastic about Pincus as an investigator who would bring them financial opportunity, apparently did not attach much significance to his work. Pincus, however, remained confident.

Sanger did not have trouble persuading McCormick to support Pincus's research. McCormick remembered Roy Hoskins from her work with the Neuroendocrine Research Institute, and he was now a director of the Worcester Foundation. On June 8, 1953, McCormick visited the Worcester Foundation with Sanger and Mrs. Hoskins. Before she left, the aging philanthropist pledged $10,000 a year to the Foundation. She was quite willing to increase the pledge as Pincus presented her with new budgets, and for the remaining 14 years of her life, she contributed most generously. Her will provided one million dollars to the foundation.

Pincus chose John Rock, a Catholic gynecologist and a professor at Harvard Medical School, to head the clinical studies. Rock already had some experience with the use of progesterone in the treatment of human infertility. As he treated women with gynecological problems, he would simultaneously obtain information about the hormone's role in human contraception. Sanger at first opposed the choice because of Rock's religion, but Pincus did not give in to her. Rock's medical practice, plus the growing problem of population increase, had convinced him that birth control was necessary. McCormick, who agreed to supply the funds, spent a considerable amount of time with Rock to familiarize herself with his work.

Seeking a regimen that would imitate the patient's normal menstrual cycle, Rock took Pincus's suggestion to give progesterone for 20 successive days, beginning on the fifth day of the cycle. The results showed that progesterone produced the desired inhibition. The large dose required produced undesirable side effects, however, and was expensive.

Searle had supplied Pincus and his group with a series of

synthesized compounds closely related to progesterone. Animal tests identified some that suppressed ovulation very effectively and were active at relatively low doses when given orally.

Rock and his colleagues found that one of these named norethynodrel proved very satisfactory. Superior to progesterone in suppressing monthly ovulation, it also caused fewer side effects. That the suppression of ovulation was temporary became clear when some of Rock's patients later conceived. It was fortuitous that one batch of norethynodrel contained minute amounts of an estrogenic substance named mestranol. This accident led to the discovery that the inclusion of estrogen had the desirable effect of decreasing breakthrough bleeding.

The decision was made to add a specific amout of estrogen to the progesterone-like component, and Enovid-10® thus became the first birth control pill. Incidentally, by 1945 there was sufficient evidence for Harvard's noted physician-investigator Fuller Albright to suggest using estrogen as an oral contraceptive. The idea was ignored at the time, however, perhaps because of fear of serious untoward effects from estrogen.

When the Fifth International Planned Parenthood Federation Conference was held in Tokyo in 1955, Pincus and Chang presented their findings, with McCormick paying their expenses. Rock refused to go because he believed that more data were needed before they made a public presentation.

Large-scale testing, still on an experimental basis, was begun in Puerto Rico in 1956. Use of the drug was not legal in Massachusetts at that date because it was primarily aimed at preventing conception, not treating infertility or some other gynecological disorder. Through Dr. Edris Rice-Wray, a faculty member at Puerto Rico Medical School and director of the Puerto Rico Family Planning Association, 100 married mothers were recruited for the study. These women lived in a new housing project near San Juan. A large percentage of the original volunteers dropped out, but their places were quickly taken by other women eager to avoid pregnancy.

Additional trial sites were found, and eventually thousands of women participated in the field testing. At the invitation of President Jean-Claude Duvalier, the project was taken to Haiti.

Katharine Dexter McCormick, 1963
Courtesy of the Massachusetts
Institute of Technology Museum

In the United States, sites for similar projects included Norfolk (Virginia) General Hospital, Fitzsimons Army Hospital in Denver, West Virginia University School of Medicine in Morgantown, and the Los Angeles Planned Parenthood Center.

The results indicated that Enovid was effective and safe, although it was debatable that sufficient time had passed before the evaluations were made. There was still no assurance that a serious condition might not surface later.

In 1960 the U.S. Food and Drug Administration approved Enovid as an oral contraceptive. Prior to that, Pincus and his wife had traveled to many countries to promote the pill, thanks to McCormick's support. By 1975, 50 million women throughout the world were using the pill. Over the years there have been modifications of both dosage and composition of the pill, and much more information about side effects is available. But oral contraceptives remain not only very effective but also very popular.

McCormick's philanthropy also extended to MIT. "Since my graduation in 1904," she wrote, "I have wished to express my gratitude to the Institute for its advanced policy of scientific education for women." Thus her interest was comfortable housing for women students at MIT. (She was determined that admission would not be denied because of lack of dormitory space.) Stanley McCormick Hall West and East, accommodating 362 students, were built in the 1960s.

The victim of a stroke, McCormick died in Boston in 1967 at the age of 92. Planned Parenthood was not forgotten—her will provided that the organization receive five million dollars. Today the Katharine Dexter McCormick Library is an important part of the Planned Parenthood Federation of America.

In 1991 feminist Peg Yorkin established a ten million dollar endowment for the Feminist Majority Foundation. A priority of the fund was to bring RU 486, the abortifacient developed in France, or a similar drug, to the United States. McCormick's example has not been forgotten.

In 1968, James R. Killian, Jr., then chairman of the corporation, Massachusetts Institute of Technology, made this public acknowledgment: "[Mrs. McCormick] was a great lady, self-disciplined, steadfast in principle, decisive in judgment, firm in adhering to her own ideas and taste, and withal instinctively gracious and generous."

But perhaps a more fitting tribute to McCormick is the dedication of Gregory Pincus's *The Control of Fertility*: "This book is dedicated to Mrs. Stanley McCormick because of her steadfast faith in scientific inquiry and her unswerving encouragement of human dignity."

Chapter 9

Betty Friedan

Women must be educated to a new integration of roles.
—Betty Friedan, 1963

Betty Friedan is an acknowledged leader of women's liberation. For her, there was never any doubt that this included access to contraception and abortion.

Friedan was born in Peoria, Illinois, on February 4, 1921, to Harry and Miriam (Horwitz) Goldstein. Betty Naomi, as they named her, was the first of three children. Miriam Goldstein, who was well educated, had edited what was known as the woman's page of a newspaper. (Today it would appear under some euphemism such as Life Styles Section.) Harry Goldstein was an immigrant and a Jew—a successful man who became the owner of a jewelry store. The family lived comfortably but experienced discrimination; Jews were not welcome in high school sororities or at the local country club for example. Miriam Goldstein's discontent was also a deterrent to family harmony; she regretted losing her job and would have liked her husband to earn more.
Friedan was a good student, the valedictorian of her high school class. By 1942 she had graduated summa cum laude from Smith College. Her chosen field was psychology, which led to graduate school at the University of California in Berkeley. She did not, however, stay long enough to earn a degree.
Friedan's next move was to New York City, where she lived in Greenwich Village and worked for a labor news service. In

117

these days, she sometimes arranged for a Smith alumna to have an abortion because, as she recalls, "I was a radical, also a psychologist and unshockable."

Veterans returning from World War II often displaced from their jobs women who had held these positions "for the duration." Betty Friedan was one of these displaced women, but she managed to find somewhere else to work.

In June 1947, Betty married Carl Friedan, who had run the Soldier Show Company in Europe and was a producer of summer theater in New Jersey. When her first child was born in 1949, Friedan took maternity leave. Five years later she again requested maternity leave. This time she was replaced, and her replacement was a man. She has termed her anger at the situation the first personal stirring of her own feminism. It is interesting to note that some 40 years later, President Clinton signed the Family Leave Act. Although not aimed exclusively at maternity leave, this law does address such a situation.

Carl Friedan in time became an advertising executive. There were eventually three children in the family—Daniel would become a theoretical physicist; Jonathan, an engineer; and Emily, a public-health pediatrician. Friedan has always taken great pride in her children, regarding them as one of the basic satisfactions of her life. By 1957, when the Cold War was in the forefront of international relations, the Friedans settled in an 11-room Victorian house on the Hudson River in Rockland County. Betty Friedan did freelance articles for magazines.

That year Friedan circulated a questionnaire among her classmates who had graduated 15 years earlier from Smith College. Two hundred women, 89 percent of them housewives, answered questions about their life experiences and feelings since leaving their alma mater.

This was an era of prosperity in the business world and of large families with a stay-home mother on the domestic front. The questionnaires revealed that many of these women were unhappy with their situations; their lives were empty and they found little to look forward to. For these affluent and educated women, a husband, children, and a beautiful home were not enough; they were not content to live vicariously through their spouses and children. Friedan realized that the image of a well-off American housewife glorified by advertisements and fiction was a deception. Later she would refer to this illusion as the "feminine mystique."

At first Friedan attempted to present her findings in a magazine article, but the male editor of *McCall's* rejected it. The *Ladies' Home Journal* changed the article so much that she refused to allow it to run. *Redbook* turned it down, believing that only a very neurotic housewife would identify with the spiritual malaise described.

Now Friedan saw the opportunity before her—she would write a book on this subject. Aided by her knowledge of psychology, she carefully analyzed the data from the returned questionnaires. Originally she intended to take about a year to complete her book, which she decided to call *The Feminine Mystique.* She used the resources of the New York Public Library, where she would sometimes write at a carrel. If it was quiet, she might work at home. But the actual writing was only part of the task she had set for herself.

Friedan sought the opinions of psychologists, physicians, clergy, and others who should understand human behavior. Of course the book was also a mirror of her own life and reactions. She had hoped to finish the manuscript in one year, but Norton did not publish *The Feminine Mystique* until 1963.

The book was a bestseller and soon was translated into several languages other than English. The numerous anecdotal descriptions added up to a portrayal of women leading lives of quiet desperation. There was intense regret over unfulfilled potential, unfinished education, missed career opportunities, and other issues in a period when marriage was considered the essence of female existence.

Scores of letters poured in, reassuring Friedan that many readers were identifying with the persons portrayed. One typical comment was "So long as I can think of attaining future education, . . . the future seems exhilarating."

But the book was controversial. Among its severe critics were women unwilling to admit that many of their sisters needed to find individual identity; some people felt that most nonaffluent

Betty Friedan, late 1950s
Courtesy of the Schlesinger Library, Radcliffe College

women were too occupied with everyday living to have such feelings. In that Cold War period, when fear of the Soviet Union seemed to dominate everything, Friedan was accused of being "more of a threat to the United States than the Russians."

By 1964 the Friedans moved back to New York City because the children were no longer welcome in carpools and Friedan "couldn't stand being a freak alone in the suburbs any longer." She continued, however, to publicize her thesis through radio and television interviews as well as speaking engagements throughout the country.

Friedan's fame brought a new opportunity: for five years she taught the writing of nonfiction at New York University and the

New School for Social Research. During this time she was also seeking material for another book about women's lives. That book never materialized, but interviews with many women who had problems convinced her that enforcement of existing laws (with regard to sex discrimination in the work place) and new legislation (such as the legalization of abortion) were necessary to women's liberation.

To implement these views, Friedan founded in October 1966 an important civil rights group known as the National Organization for Women (NOW). The original statement of purpose, of which she was the author, was accepted with one exception: the call for access to birth control and abortion was deleted because it was considered too controversial. In 1967, however, the organization's bill of rights included the right of a woman to control her reproductive life.

The National Organization for Women has grown into the largest women's rights organization in the United States. Members are actively involved in every issue relating to full equality for women in society. The organization has adopted the following stand on reproductive rights:

> NOW affirms that [reproductive rights] are issues of life and death for women, not mere matters of choice. NOW supports access to safe and legal abortion, to effective birth control, to reproductive health and education. We oppose attempts to restrict these rights through legislation, regulation or Constitutional amendment.

In 1968, Friedan co-founded the National Conference for Repeal of Abortion Laws. After the Supreme Court's 1973 decision on abortion, this organization changed its name to the National Abortion Rights Action League (NARAL). It remains an effective and vocal force in maintaining legal rights relating to abortion.

Friedan was NOW's first president and continued in that office until 1970, when she refused reelection. There were power struggles in NOW, and radical feminists often did not agree with Friedan, who was considered difficult. In particular, she showed less interest than some of her cohorts in lesbian rights, warring with men, and others issues. She once explained, "If we define our movement in antilove, antichild terms, we are not going to have the power of the women and the help of increasing numbers of men who can identify their liberation with women's liberation."

The fiftieth anniversary of women's suffrage—August 20, 1970—was the occasion of a national women's strike for equality. Instigated by Friedan, it was the largest turnout for women's rights in half a century and did much to impress people throughout the nation with the growing influence of the women's movement. Friedan was one of the 25,000 who marched in New York City.

During the 1970s and 1980s, Friedan involved herself with psychology, sociology, and women's history. Her second book, *It Changed My Life: Writings on the Women's Movement*, came out in 1976. Her next book, published in 1981, was *The Second Stage*. Here she called for flexible work schedules, parental leave, child care, and new housing arrangements. Her suggestion that feminists should consider the importance of love, family, and home in their lives was not well received by "victims of rape, violence and unpaid domestic labor," to quote one woman.

Friedan also differed with many feminists in coming to terms with the major differences between men and women. She said in 1986, "There has to be a concept of equality that takes into account that women are the ones who have babies. Why should the law treat us like male clones?"

Friedan's own life had changed drastically since the days of what some termed "The Fabulous Fifties." After considering divorce for years, she obtained a final decree in 1969 and was then concerned with supporting her children. Admitting to being lonely, she started a "weekend commune," where her friends met on weekends and holidays for about ten years.

For many years Friedan's consuming interest was the Equal Rights Amendment (ERA), introduced in 1972. The substance of this amendment is expressed in its Section 1:

> Equality of rights under the law shall not be denied or abridged by the United States or by any State on account of sex.

The proposed amendment required ratification by 38 states. By the first deadline, three states were still needed. Congress extended the deadline for three years, to a total of ten, but to no avail; by June 30, 1982, the amendment was dead.

Friedan believed that NOW was partially responsible for this failure. According to her, "The sexual politics that disturbed the sense of priorities of the women's movement during the 1970s made it easy for the so-called Moral Majority to lump ERA with homosexual rights and abortion into one explosive package of licentious, family-threatening sex."

A world traveler, Friedan has attended women's conferences sponsored by the United Nations and has visited with such personages as Simone de Beauvoir, Indira Ghandi, Jihan Sadat, and Pope Paul VI. At home, she is active in the Democratic Party.

Friedan's fourth book, *The Fountain of Age*, reflects the interest she developed in gerontology. (She is affiliated with the Andrus Gerontology Center at the University of Southern California, where she has been a distinguished visiting professor.) She believes that the age mystique denies old people their "personhood" in the same way that the feminine mystique denied women theirs. So far as Friedan herself is concerned, she says she is moving into old age with a good deal of exhilaration. She will continue to enjoy her grandchildren, to read mysteries and science fiction, and to create exotic soups.

The effect of the women's movement, in which Friedan played so dominant a part, is seen everywhere today. Fulltime housewives are relatively rare as more and more women join the work force. They have entered professions and occupations where they were once shunned—politics, the ministry, the military, finance, and law enforcement, to name a few. At the same time, the issue of child care has become more acute, and the need for abortion on demand is more pressing.

Lawrence Tribe, an authority on constitutional law, believes that *The Feminine Mystique* was a powerful force behind the political empowerment of women in support of abortion rights. He also credits Friedan for exerting great personal influence on those who pushed for and won a favorable Supreme Court decision.

Chapter 10

Sarah Weddington

A basic tenet of pro-choice is that women have the right
to control what occurs in their own bodies.
                                —Roger Rosenblatt, 1990

The fundamental moral issue is whether or not what's being killed is a human being.
                                —Judge Robert Bork, 1990

Two 1973 United States Supreme Court decisions that legalized abortion played a significant role in the emancipation of
American women. These decisions evolved through the contributions of many people, but one of the most important was a young
woman named Sarah Weddington who argued the more important case, *Roe v. Wade*, before the Supreme Court and won it.

Sarah Weddington was born in Abilene, Texas, on February
5, 1945, one of several children. Her parents were Lena (Mor-
rison) Ragle and Herbert Doyle Ragle. Since Herbert Ragle was
a Methodist minister, the family made frequent moves from one
small town to another in west Texas. Here Sarah rode horseback
on the vast plains and wondered about the world beyond, a world
that she would soon experience. As a minister's daughter, she did
what was expected; she played the organ and piano, was a youth
leader, and engaged in other activities that she later credited with
giving her confidence in herself. She was a hard worker, an independent thinker, and a determined young woman. In her
youth, marriage and children were not high on her list of priorities.

At McMurry College in Abilene, Sarah Weddington enrolled in the secondary school education curriculum, specializing in teaching English and speech. But her sights were set on law school. In June 1965, Weddington was one of five women among 120 men entering the University of Texas School of Law. She did well, graduating in 1967 in the top quarter of her class. Her first job was working for one of her professors, who under the American Bar Association's auspices was responsible for making proposed revisions of ethical standards for lawyers.

In August 1968, Sarah married Ronald Weddington, who was just beginning law school in Austin after military service. The year before, when she found she was pregnant, they had crossed the border at Eagle Pass so she could have an abortion in Mexico. This was illegal there, as it was in Texas, except to save the mother's life. Apparently the Mexican law was not enforced, however. Although the procedure went without mishap, Weddington did not forget the incident.

While her husband was in law school, Weddington became part of the women's movement by joining a consciousness-raising group. The women read—and some wrote for—*The Rag,* Austin's underground, counterculture newspaper that provided information about contraception and abortion. One of the prime movers was Judy Smith, a graduate student. Smith and other members of the group were trying to find places where safe abortions were provided by competent doctors. Weddington's contribution was doing legal research on Texas law.

It was not known if the volunteers in the referral center could be prosecuted, and that remained an ongoing concern. They took heart in the fact that ministers and rabbis in various parts of the country were part of the Clergy Consultative Service on Abortion, which helped women get safe operations.

There were now cases in federal courts challenging the anti-abortion laws of several states. Some laws, such as the Texas one, were termed restrictive. If abortion were permitted in cases of rape, incest, fetal deformity, or to save the mother's life or health, the law was designated liberalized. Maryland had such a law. In California and New York abortion was legal. Weddington followed the challenges with interest.

One day Judy Smith urged that a lawsuit at the federal level be brought against the state of Texas because of its antiabortion law. Her suggestion was prompted by a recent case involving *The Rag*. When the Regents of the University of Texas banned the sale of that paper on campus, a suit brought against the University of Texas reached the United States Supreme Court and was won by the plaintiffs. Smith expressed the hope that Weddington would take the proposed abortion case on a *pro bono* basis. She had found no one willing to do it without recompense, she wanted a woman lawyer, and she was impressed with Weddington's research on abortion law.

Weddington was receptive to the idea, especially since she had had personal experience with illegal abortion. She now had some extra time and had access to the law library of the University of Texas. Moreover, she knew friends and also some professors sympathetic to the cause who would be willing to work on this project that would of necessity be run on a shoestring. Because of the suits filed by other states, Weddington assumed it unlikely that Texas's suit would be singled out for argument before the Supreme Court. It would, however, add strength to the other challenges.

Weddington decided to seek the help of her former law school classmate, Linda Coffee of Dallas. Coffee was familiar with federal lawsuits, having worked as a clerk for the well-known Texan, Federal District Judge Sarah Hughes. Coffee was definitely interested and her firm raised no objections. She, along with Weddington, wanted to help the various women who contacted the referral center when they needed reliable information about abortions. Technically, however, these women were not strong as potential plaintiffs.

One plaintiff chosen was a woman whom they named Jane Roe; she had been referred to Coffee by a lawyer friend. Roe was pregnant and wanted an abortion. Single and 21, she worked as a waitress and would be fired when her pregnancy became known, but she lacked the resources to go to another state to terminate the pregnancy. As Roe's pregnancy advanced, her lawyers decided to call for a class-action suit. This ensured that in the event of a favorable verdict, even if Roe were no longer pregnant, the verdict would hold for others. (Roe had the baby, which she put up for adoption.)

Later Roe made known her real name. She also disclosed that her story that she had been gang-raped was fabricated. Weddington and Coffee made no mention of the rape in the document filed, however. They hoped to get a broader verdict than, for example, one that permitted abortion when there had been rape. Their aim was twofold: to have the restrictive Texas law declared unconstitutional and to prohibit the prosecution of physicians who performed abortions.

The other plaintiffs were a husband and wife who feared pregnancy because of a health problem of the wife. This couple was ultimately judged to lack standing—in other words, the man and woman were not appropriate plaintiffs.

The case *Roe v. Wade* was named for Jane Roe and for Henry Wade, the district attorney of Dallas County. Coffee filed for *Roe* in March 1970, in Dallas and personally paid the required fee. A three-judge panel heard the case in May. The next month, a panel ruled the Texas law on abortion unconstitutional.

Since there was still no specific restriction on the prosecution of doctors, Weddington and Coffee appealed directly to the United States Supreme Court. Their thinking was that as long as Wade was still free to prosecute physicians, members of the medical profession would be less likely to perform abortions. On May 21, 1971, they learned that their case, along with one involving Georgia law, would be heard.

With Ron now a lawyer, the Weddingtons lived briefly in Fort Worth, where Sarah was assistant city attorney. The Supreme Court case needed much study, so the couple moved back to Austin to start their own practice. There they would be less isolated and have valuable contacts.

Preparing the brief was a tremendous task that required the expertise and efforts of many volunteers dedicated to obtaining reproductive rights for women. Necessary expenses were paid by a few generous contributors who were of the same persuasion.

The *Roe* brief was filed August 17, 1971. Oral arguments were presented December 13 by Weddington, then 26. Her co-counsel was Coffee. Weddington's proud mother came to Washington to be present to hear her daughter. Bent on hearing history made, Betty Friedan was also there to listen.

A companion case to *Roe* was *Doe v. Bolton*. Mary Doe was the pseudonym of a mother of three living in Atlanta, Georgia, where state law allowed abortion only for medical necessity, birth defects, and in rape cases. When Doe was pregnant with her fourth child, she wanted an abortion because the family was so poor and because she had once been a patient in a mental hospital. According to Georgia law, abortions had to be done in an accredited hospital. The patient had to be a resident of Georgia, and the advance approval of three physicians as well as a hospital committee were necessary. Turned down by a local public hospital, Doe tried the Legal Aid Society. When her plight became known to four women lawyers, a class-action suit was initiated to challenge the burdensome Georgia law; it was argued before the Supreme Court by Margie Pitts Hames.

Victory came on January 22, 1973. With regard to *Roe*, the justices decreed the Texas law unconstitutional: the plaintiff had a right to an abortion done during the first trimester by a licensed person. The Supreme Court also ruled that after the first trimester, the state may regulate abortion and after fetal viability, the state may forbid abortion except to save the mother.

The judgment about the first trimester depended on the right of privacy, which was of special importance to Weddington. This phrase does not appear in the Constitution, but in 1928 Justice Louis Brandeis stated:

> The makers of our Constitution undertook to secure conditions favorable to the pursuit of happiness. . . . They sought to protect Americans in their beliefs, their thoughts, their emotions and their sensations. They conferred, as against the government, the right to be let alone—the most comprehensive of rights and the right most valued by civilized men.

The verdict on *Doe v. Bolton* was that the Georgia law was unconstitutional because the procedural guidelines made abortions unnecessarily difficult to obtain. Sometimes the term *Roe v. Wade* is used to cover the two cases.

Doe's child was put up for adoption. Later mother and

daughter met. Doe is now a prolife advocate but the daughter believes that her biological mother had a right to obtain an abortion.

It is worth considering briefly at this point how thinking and legislation on abortion have evolved, particularly with reference to Britain and the United States.

Abortion, deliberately induced, has been known for centuries. For instance, the Hippocratic Oath includes this promise: "I will not give to a woman a pessary to induce abortion." Hippocrates is believed to have lived 460–377 B.C. Exemplifying a different viewpoint, Plato and Aristotle did not oppose abortion under certain conditions. The Greeks even practiced infanticide at times, particularly if newborns were females.

Exodus 21: 22–25 provides for the punishment of a person who strikes a pregnant woman, thereby causing her to abort. This is in keeping with the philosophy of the ancient Hittite, Sumerian, Assyrian, and Persian cultures. The Romans condemned abortion—for example, in the first century, the sellers of abortifacients were penalized. Christianity, bolstered by the belief that life is bestowed by God, was emphatically antiabortion.

Physicians meeting in London in 1756 agreed that abortion to save a woman's life was permitted. According to British common law, which is evolved by judges, abortion was illegal after "quickening," the time when fetal movement was first felt by the mother. This occurs between the sixteenth and eighteenth weeks of pregnancy. Since pregnancy tests were unknown until 1927, a woman could not be sure she was pregnant until she felt "life" because cessation of menstruation occurs in conditions other than pregnancy.

In 1803 the atmosphere in Britain changed and the law provided that abortion before quickening was subject to such measures as exile to a penal colony, whipping, or imprisonment. After quickening, the punishment could be death. Thirty-five years later, this law was softened. Then an 1861 law mandated prison terms for persons securing "unlawful" abortions—and this included the woman directly involved. There was no definition of "unlawful."

By 1929 Parliament had ruled that the abortion of a viable fetus was not unlawful if the operation were done in good faith to preserve the mother's life. In 1938 a ruling implied that according to circumstances, a doctor may be duty-bound to end a pregnancy. Finally, the British Abortion Act of 1967 made abortion on demand a reality, but required the certification of two physicians. This act does not apply to Northern Ireland, where the 1861 law is in effect. Interpretation of the 1929 British law has made 28 weeks the upper limit of the period when abortion may be performed. The 1967 law became something of a model for other countries seeking to liberalize their abortion policy.

In the American colonies there were no written laws against abortion. Under common law, abortion was legal until quickening. In the event that an abortion was performed after quickening, the woman was not prosecuted. The first statute was enacted by Connecticut in 1821. This forbade the administration of poison to bring about abortion after quickening. At the time, it was believed that a dose large enough to kill the fetus might have a lesser effect on the mother. The state of the art in medicine was such that abortion induced by instruments was a truly risky procedure. So it is understandable that by 1840, eight states limited abortion.

Beginning in 1800 and continuing for the next 100 years, the average number of children born to white women fell dramatically. As we have seen, birth control was becoming more common. During this period, abortion advertising flourished, and the presumption is that the advertising was effective. For example, "female monthly pills" were recommended to restore "blocked menses." Madame Restell (see Chapter 3) arranged for an operation in the event that her medicine failed. Many of the products advertised were, of course, useless. Worse, some were dangerous.

The health of the mother was therefore a legitimate concern. And there was a desire on the part of physicians to end the taking of quack nostrums and other substances. Also, some doctors, remembering the Hippocratic Oath, were hesitant to become involved in abortions. Thus it is not surprising that the newly formed American Medical Association in 1857 began a movement that tended to prohibit abortion. Two years later the AMA put restrictions on abortions before quickening.

Lawrence Tribe points out in his book on abortion that other issues were involved in the AMA's position. One was nativism. After midcentury, the birth rate among Catholics, many of whom were immigrants, exceeded that of native-born Protestants. Some members of the medical profession attributed this largely to abortion, frequently resorted to by Protestants but seldom used by Catholics. In addition, the AMA's Committee on Criminal Abortion did not want to see women gain so much control of their lives; a person who had an abortion was "unmindful of the course marked out for her by Providence. . . . She sinks into old age like a withered tree, stripped of its foliage; with the stain of blood upon her soul."

We recall that in 1873, as part of the Comstock antiobscenity act, the federal government banned access to information about abortion as well as contraception. The second part of the nineteenth century saw also increased antiabortion legislation at the state level. Quickening now received little consideration. In general, therapeutic abortion was allowed, provided one or more physicians deemed it necessary to save the mother's life. By the beginning of this century, each of the 48 states forbade the use of drugs or instruments to bring about abortion, but an exception was allowed when, in the opinion of a doctor, the woman's life was at stake.

In 1869 the Catholic church under Pope Pius IX decreed excommunication to all who aborted. Christian doctrine historically opposed abortion, in the belief that life is bestowed by God, not man. However, it is interesting that at the time, the medical profession appeared to be a greater influence than the church. In the twentieth century, abortion became safer as antibiotics and blood banks were developed. The United States was no longer an agricultural nation that prized large families, and after the Depression occurred it was clear that just one more child in a family could impose considerable hardship. By the second half of the century, women were more liberated; led by Betty Friedan, Gloria Steinem, and others, they knew the truth of Margaret Sanger's contention that no woman could call herself free until she controlled her own reproduction.

Some doctors were now finding fetal deformity, rape, and

even poverty sufficient reasons for abortion. In contrast to the thinking of physicians in the previous century, they were seeking less regulation in determining when to perform abortions. In the 1960s, fetal deformities caused by the drug thalidomide and by German measles (before vaccination was available)* focused attention on the fact that in many states, fetal deformity did not justify legal abortion because the mother's life was not in jeopardy.

In 1959 the American Law Institute (ALI), whose membership included both practicing and academic lawyers, drew up a standard abortion code that would become a model. It upheld abortion when pregnancy "would gravely impair the physical and mental health of the mother" and if it were likely that the child would be born with "grave physical or mental defects." The code also permitted abortion when pregnancy resulted from rape or incest. The approval of two physicians was required.

Roger Rosenblatt observes that it was always men who made the decisions about abortion, though they were unlikely to suffer the consequences. Laurence Tribe makes the point that laws restricting abortion reduce women's ability to function in society as equals of males.

Some divisions of organized religion expressed a positive attitude towards abortion; for example, in 1967 the American Episcopal bishops lent support to liberalizing abortion laws. A year later the American Baptist convention followed.

By 1973, the year of *Roe*, 13 states had passed laws based on the ALI Code, while 15 legislatures were considering them. Since that time, the courts have protected the individual in various other areas related to reproduction. *Griswold v. Connecticut* challenged a Connecticut law prohibiting the use of contraceptives. The ruling in 1965 was that the right of married couples to use contraceptives falls within the zone of privacy created by several fundamental guarantees of the Constitution.

Sherri Finkbine, a television personality who had taken the drug thalidomide while pregnant, had to go to Sweden to have an abortion. In 1970 an obstetrician named Jane Hodgson performed an abortion on a 23-year-old mother who had contracted German measles while pregnant. Dr. Hodgson was arrested and tried for this. Later Roe invalidated the Minnesota law, thus overturning her conviction.

Seven years later, in *Eisenstadt v. Baird*, the Supreme Court ruled that Massachusetts could not prohibit the distribution of contraceptives to unmarried persons, stating that if "the right of privacy means anything, it is the right of the individual, married or single, to be free from unwarranted governmental intrusion into matters so fundamentally affecting a person as the decision whether to bear or beget a child."

The two landmark decisions, *Roe* and *Doe*, not only made early abortion on demand valid in the United States but contributed to a widening rift between those who uphold the right to abortion and those who oppose it. The Supreme Court itself has acknowledged: "Abortion raises moral and spiritual questions over which honorable persons can disagree sincerely and profoundly."

A Harris poll in June 1990 posed the question: "Do you favor or oppose giving a woman, with the advice of her physician, the right to choose to have an abortion?" Seventy-five percent answered that she should have that right. Apparently the majority of Americans agree with *Roe v. Wade*.

For those who want to keep abortion available as an option, reproductive freedom is a basic human right, and thus a woman's right to control what happens to her body is paramount. While there is recognition that the developing embryo has the potential for life, abortion is not considered murder. Abortion is not deemed a primary method of birth control but looked on as a backup in case of contraceptive failure. Some who support the right to abortion are concerned with world population; others are concerned with the quality of life to the extent that they believe it is an act of mercy to abort a fetus known to have serious untreatable disease. Abortion rights activists do not support forced abortion; they believe that a woman should have the choice to have or to refuse an abortion. They also reason that it is wrong for their opponents to try to impose their beliefs on those who do not see abortion as immoral. Feminists, in particular, bitterly resent such interference.

Right to Life advocates believe strongly that the weak and innocent should be protected, not obliterated. They try, particularly with visual images of fetuses, to convince others that a young embryo within the uterus deserves the same treatment as a baby who has been delivered from the uterus.

John Willke, M.D., known for years for his antiabortion stance, was once asked what abortion means. His reply illustrates the essential thinking of the Right to Life movement:

> It is a simple fact, proven for more than a hundred years, that what grows within the mother is living, is human, is already a boy or a girl, is complete and intact already at the first-cell stage. This is a human life growing within her. When you destroy this human life, the accurate biologic word for this is *kill*.

Right to Lifers favor using informed consent laws that force prospective candidates for abortion to look at pictures of the developing fetus. Since they advocate adoption, they work to help such organizations as Birthright. (See page 136 for information about Birthright.)

There have been several legal challenges to *Roe*. In 1976 in *Planned Parenthood of Central Missouri v. Danforth*, the Supreme Court held that parental and spousal consent requirements were unconstitutional. A 1980 case, *Harris v. McRae*, challenged the Hyde Amendment, which bans Medicaid funds for abortion except when necessary to save the woman's life. The justices found the Hyde Amendment constitutional. In 1992 *Planned Parenthood of Southeastern Pennsylvania v. Casey* challenged Pennsylvania's 1989 Abortion Control Act. This law required that except in defined emergencies (a) a woman must wait 24 hours between consenting to and receiving an abortion; (b) the woman must be given state-mandated information on abortion and be offered state-authorized literature about fetal development; (c) a married woman must inform her husband that she intends to have an abortion; and (d) minors seeking abortion must have the consent of one parent or guardian or receive a judicial waiver. The Pennsylvania law was found constitutional except in the case of (c). The court reaffirmed the validity of a woman's right to abortion according to *Roe*. The restrictions imposed by (a), (b), and (d) were found not to constitute "undue burden" to the woman involved.

PREGNANT?

and need help . . .

YOU NEED HELP?

You are pregnant — and your first thought is — "No — not me — oh, please — not me!"
You are scared . . . resentful . . . angry.
Your whole world is changing and you don't want to face it. Not now — not yet.
You want yesterday again.
Who will listen and really understand how upset you are? BIRTHRIGHT!

WHAT AM I GOING TO DO?

— How can I be sure I am pregnant?
— How should I tell my family?
— Can I continue in school? . . . keep my job?
— Where can I obtain good medical care?

— What about finances?
— Can I keep my baby?
— Is marriage the solution?
— Where can I live until my baby is born?

HOW DO WE HELP YOU?)

Anonymous pregnancy test
Education guidance
Shelter home
Community resource information
Maternity clothes/layettes

Medical care
Legal advice
Help with job placement
Referral for professional counseling
Adoption information

. . . And other ways depending on your particular circumstances. We help you to think about your future and that of your baby and give you as much or as little assistance as you need or desire.

Birthright cares about you. We know you are facing perhaps the greatest personal crisis of your life. You don't have to face it alone.

TRUST US

Don't be pressured into abortion by your friends, family or doctor. Birthright offers the alternative to abortion.

Birthright is staffed by trained volunteers and operates on financial donations by individuals and organizations. Birthright is independent; non-political, non-sectarian and prepared to help you whether you are single or married, regardless of age, race or religion. Our help is free and confidential.

Give life a chance and we'll help you every step of the way.

NO QUESTIONS ASKED — NO JUDGMENT MADE — NO STRINGS ATTACHED

CALL OR CONTACT BIRTHRIGHT

FREE & CONFIDENTIAL
PREGNANCY SERVICES
800-848-LOVE (U.S.)
(5683)

An advertisement for Birthright.

In 1992 *Time* magazine compared the situation as it existed in the United States to that in several other countries. In Canada, China, France, Italy and Japan, abortion is legal, subject to certain restrictions. In keeping with China's one-child-per-family policy, the state can demand abortion. Egypt has an official policy that makes abortion illegal unless the woman's life is in jeopardy; some private facilities may, however, do the procedure. In Canada, China, France and Italy, the government covers the cost; the Japanese government does not. The consent required varies from country to country.

In 1993 Poland enacted a law that restricts abortions to situations where the mother's life or health is threatened, when pregnancy is the result of rape or incest, or when prenatal testing shows the fetus to be seriously, irreparably damaged. All abortions must be performed in public health centers. Doctors who violate the law face up to two years in prison.

Until the 1992 presidential election, American advocates of abortion rights had great concern that with changing membership of the Supreme Court, *Roe* might be overturned. With the election of President Clinton, this is not likely to happen in the near future. He has declared himself prochoice and no doubt will appoint justices receptive to what *Roe* represents.

Both camps would like a constitutional amendment regarding abortion, one side desiring protection for reproductive rights and the other protection for the fetus. A Constitutional amendment must be proposed either by a two-thirds majority in each house of Congress or by a constitutional convention called at the request of the legislatures of three-fourths of the states. The amendment must be ratified by the legislatures of three-fourths of the states or by conventions in three-fourths of the states, as ordered by Congress. Neither side is likely to get an amendment under these conditions.

Because individual states may act through their legislatures to pass laws about abortion (see page 138), the result could be an undesirable patchwork of laws.

The divisiveness caused by the very emotional issue of abortion is serious. True compromise will be difficult for those who are convinced that abortion is murder. They are also not likely to be

Abortion foes revamp consent bill

LANSING, Mich. (AP) — Abortion foes offered Thursday a revamped bill requiring women to wait 24 hours and be given fetal drawings before having an abortion as they launched a second try at passing the measure.

Rep. Jessie Dalman said the measure is similar to one that died in a conference committee in December, but predicted its chances of passage are better because backers plan to bill it as protection for women.

"It's a sensitive bill. It meets the needs of women and treats those who are considering abortion with respect and concern and compassion and I don't think that was ever shown before," said Dalman, R-Holland.

"The perception was that it was a harsh bill and it's not a harsh bill."

A pro-choice lawmaker said the talk about compassion is only an attempt to disguise the real goal to make it harder to get abortions.

"It is still parental consent for adult women, with the state acting in loco parentis," said Rep. Maxine Berman, D-Southfield.

"The only purpose of this bill is to try to terrorize women out of the decision to terminate a pregnancy. It doesn't empower anybody."

The bill originally passed by the Senate in February 1992 required women to view photographs of developing fetuses and be given information about the risks of abortion, as well as wait 24 hours before having an abortion.

House members objected to the photographs, however. In a rare setback for abortion foes in Michigan, the bill died after no compromise could be worked out.

"The issue of the pictures has been one that is very controversial. All the way through the battle we were told that we were going to mandate women to look at bloody fetuses. That has not been true, that has not been the intent from day one," said Sen. Jack Welborn, R-Kalamazoo.

The new version would require women be given drawings of fetuses that are used in a controversial state health course, the Michigan Model for Comprehensive School Health Education. Women wouldn't be required to look at them, however.

"If they want to trash can them when they get home, that's their option," Welborn said.

Drawings are little different from the pictures the House already has rejected, Berman said.

"I also think it's a double agenda here, to use Michigan Model drawings so that those who oppose the Michigan Model can turn around and say, 'How can we show our children the same pictures being shown to women having abortions?' It's a rather transparent ploy," she said.

The bill also would allow women to get information about the risks of abortion and the fetal drawings from a doctor other than one at the abortion clinic. That would be to avoid placing an undue burden on women living far from abortion clinics.

A newspaper article that describes maneuvering to pass abortion legislation at the state level. From *The Mining Journal*, Marquette, Michigan.

Sarah Weddington
Courtesy of Sarah Weddington
She represents a saying well known in Texas:
Eternal vigilance is the price of supremacy.

receptive to the idea of setting a time during pregnancy before
which independent existence outside the uterus is not possible for
the fetus. They argue that modern technological improvements
are moving that time closer and closer to the date of conception.
There are facts to back up this assertion. Dr. Virginia Apgar,

a distinguished anesthesiologist, had long wondered "who was really responsible for the newborn." In 1952 she presented the medical world with a simple procedure that could immediately after delivery alert a doctor to any emergency needs of the infant. The Apgar Score System has been responsible for saving lives that would before 1952 have been lost. Considering that the science of neonatology today includes such procedures as intrauterine transfusion and surgery, it is reasonable enough to think that survival not possible today could be commonplace in the future.

A relatively new group named Common Cause attempts to bring both sides together to work for such things as better prenatal care programs, treatment of mothers who are substance abusers, and recruitment of more foster parents. One cofounder of Common Cause, which is active in several states, is B. J. Isaacson-Jones, whose employer is Reproductive Health Services in St. Louis, an abortion clinic. Another cofounder is Loretta Wagner, former president of Missouri Right to Life. According to Wagner, "It's possible to stand on your principles firmly, but at the same time recognize there are areas of common agreement." As individuals become less recalcitrant, they may find innovative ways to prevent unwanted pregnancy and to be of real assistance to those who have unwanted babies. With the nation's annual abortion rate at 1.6 million (representing one-fourth of all pregnancies), the need is pressing.

Weddington was elected three times to the Texas House of Representatives, serving from 1973 until 1977. Her interests included ERA, credit rights for women, maternity leave, reform of Texas's rape statutes, and equality for men and women in child custody. Weddington served the Carter administration first as general counsel to the Department of Agriculture; later as a special assistant, she advised the president on women's issues. In 1979 she became an assistant to President Carter.

With Republican administrations in power, Weddington returned to Austin, where she has a solo law practice, and also teaches at the University of Texas. Her personal life has changed since her Supreme Court case; she was divorced from Ron in 1974.

When Weddington realized that *Roe v. Wade* might be overturned, she tried to combat complacency about retaining liberal abortion laws. She has become particularly alarmed at the appointment of conservatives to the Supreme Court and has lectured throughout the country about the importance of keeping abortion open to women who want it. Her 1992 book entitled *A Question of Choice* emphasizes this point.

Numerous honors and honorary degrees have been awarded to Sarah Weddington. Most appropriately, she is a recipient of Planned Parenthood's coveted Margaret Sanger Award. Governor Ann Richards of Texas has termed Weddington's success in winning *Roe v. Wade* "one of the most important victories in history for American women."

Chapter 11

Virginia Johnson

Can [ignorance about sexual response] be allowed to con-
tinue without benefit of objective, scientific analysis?
—William H. Masters and
Virginia E. Johnson, 1966

With the advent of the contraceptive pill and the sexual
revolution, the fear of pregnancy lost its power as a deterrent to
sexual activity. There were few left who still believed that the sexual act should be reserved for procreation. At this time, William
Masters and Virginia Johnson published a scientific analysis of the
human sexual response. Using this data, they then devised ways
to treat sexual dysfunction, which they considered very common.
Later they showed their awareness of the situation in the world of
human sexuality by publishing in 1988 a very strong warning
about the consequences of irresponsible behavior in the age of
AIDS.

Virginia Johnson was born in Springfield, Missouri, on
February 11, 1925, to Herschel and Edna (Evans) Eshelman. She
was the older of two children. In 1930 the family moved to Palo
Alto, California, remaining there for three years. Then they moved
back to Missouri, where the father was a farmer.

The move from California affected young Virginia in that she
found herself ahead of her classmates and was thus able to skip
some grades. Perhaps she was less mature socially than intellec-
tually; in any event, she was left out of some of the activities of

143

her cohorts. With her sole sibling 12 years her junior, she was almost an only child and, according to her, always indulged by her elders. She read a great deal and studied piano and voice. This began what became a lifelong enjoyment for her—she still listens to classical music as she goes to sleep.

Johnson graduated from high school in 1941 at the age of 16. After a year at Drury College in Springfield, Missouri, she spent the next four years working sporadically at a clerical job in Jefferson City. Because her mother, Edna Eshelman, was active in the Republican Party, Johnson often performed at meetings of state politicians. This in turn led to employment as a country music singer for radio station KWTO in Springfield. Here she sang mezzo-soprano with a female quartet that the Gibson Coffee Company sponsored, an activity that accounts for her pseudonym at the time, Virginia Gibson.

During the 1940s, Johnson married twice. Her first marriage—a brief one—was to a politician. Her second husband was a lawyer who, unlike Johnson, did not want to have a family.

Desirous of extending her education, Virginia managed to take courses in sociology and psychology at the University of Missouri in Columbia; later she studied at the Kansas City Conservatory in St. Louis.

By 1947 Johnson was living in St. Louis, where she worked as an editorial writer and administrative secretary for the *Daily Record* until 1950. The next year she was part of the market research staff of KMOV-TV, an affiliate of Columbia Broadcasting System.

In 1950 Virginia married George V. Johnson, an engineering student at Washington University. He was also the leader of a dance band with which she sang in the early days of their marriage. When the Johnsons became the parents of two children, Scott and Lisa, Virginia left the band to stay at home full time. By 1956 the couple were divorced. Virginia's explanation was "Musicians are night people and babies are day people and I couldn't handle it all."

In 1957 Johnson began an association that would bring her fame. William Masters, a professor of clinical obstetrics and gynecology at Washington University's medical school, was looking for a female who would interview and screen volunteers for a research project involving human sexual response. He had in mind a mature, intelligent, personable woman, preferably a mother. Looking forward to completing degree requirements, Virginia had applied for an on-campus job, and in this way she became known to Masters. He picked her from a list as the best applicant.

Professionally it was an excellent choice, and over the years, these two sexologists have received numerous accolades for their work together; in fact, "Masters and Johnson" are known all over the world. Personally they have been somewhat less fortunate; they married in 1971, but divorced in 1992, when she was 67 and he 76.

Human Sexual Response by Masters and Johnson was published in 1966. It is a scientific analysis of the physiological responses of paid volunteers aged 18 to 89 — 382 women and 312 men — to various forms of sexual stimulation. To obtain actual measurements, standards methods of science, for instance, electrocardiography, were used. The investigators also employed to advantage color motion-picture photography.

Kinsey's famous studies (*Sexual Behavior in the Human Male*, 1948, and *Sexual Behavior in the Human Female*, 1953) were dependent on data obtained through direct questioning. (A more recent survey was done in 1993 by Samuel and Cynthia Janus.) The Masters-Johnson work supplied information dependent on approved instrumentation and laboratory methodology.

Human Sexual Response was a bestseller. It was in general well received by professionals such as Dr. John Rock (see Chapter 8) and Dr. Calderone. The Masters-Johnson team lectured nationwide on their book. At Johnson's suggestion, they also appeared on national television to publicize and explain their findings. (This certainly is a far cry from the atmosphere that existed under the Comstock laws.)

By January 1964, the research first begun under the aegis of Washington University School of Medicine's obstetrics and gynecology department was under the purview of the Reproductive

Biology Research Foundation. The Foundation, in addition to its research and treatment programs, trained therapists and counselors.

Human Sexual Inadequacy came out in 1970. In this book Masters and Johnson discussed the results of their counseling, which involved 510 couples. Using the knowledge gained in their previous study, they treated such conditions as impotence and vaginismus (spasms). They attained, for example, complete success with vaginismus, an 80 percent success with premature ejaculation; primary impotence was not cured in 40 percent of the cases, some of which had strong religious indoctrination. The latter results bear out the team's contention that sexual dysfunction is often a cultural disease.

The counseling technique described was unique. Dual sex-therapy teams were formed: patient and therapist were of the same sex and another therapist of the same sex as the patient's partner interpreted for the partner what the patient had divulged. Explicit instructions on sexual techniques were given for patients to practice in private during a two-week period.

The foregoing books were aimed at professionals in the field of human sexuality, although the lay public read them avidly. *The Pleasure Bond*, written by Masters and Johnson in association with Robert J. Levin, was published in 1975 for the general reading public. The authors probed the question of how a couple can strengthen the sexual relationship as time passes. According to them, the key word is commitment, and they declared their preference for monogamous relationships.

Johnson is a prolific writer, often serving as contributor as well as author and coauthor. During a magazine interview in 1993, she stated: "I like to write best when information is on the cutting edge in my mind. . . . It's exciting. I don't want to lose the thread." Masters and Johnson's books include *Homosexuality in Perspective* in 1979 and in 1988 they joined with Robert C. Kolodney, a physician, in publishing *Crisis*, a national study that showed how the AIDS virus could spread among heterosexuals. They warned about such things as defective condoms and emphasized the need for caution in choosing a partner. They called for more state and federal funding for research on the disease. Among other measures, they advocated that AIDS education begin at least by the fourth or fifth grade.

Today in retirement Johnson leads an active life in Missouri, maintaining interest in her profession, continuing to write, and enjoying her grandchildren. Among her awards and honors is one from Mary Calderone's SIECUS.

Johnson is a woman whose exceptional abilities have taken her to the top of her field without the academic degrees that some believe so essential. A fitting tribute to her career comes from Harold Lief, Professor of Psychiatry at the University of Pennsylvania's medical school, who noted in 1976 that the work of Masters and Johnson "has revolutionized not only sex therapy but also psychotherapy of people who do not have sex problems *per se*."

Epilogue

By different methods different [wo]men excel.
                                    —American proverb

During this century, women have gained control of their reproduction. Small families, spaced according to the wishes of the parents, have been beneficial, not only to countless women, but to society at large. Although the ready availability of contraception has liberated females, it has also had some unfortunate consequences.

There has been an increase in sexually transmitted diseases, which include AIDS. At present, the best hope seems to be that strong educational campaigns will stimulate the public to take proper precautions to avoid further tragedy.

A small family is one of the factors that have encouraged women to enter the work force in ever-increasing numbers, but the provision of adequate child care remains a serious and unresolved issue.

Ironically, reliable birth control methods have become associated with a great increase in the number of teenage pregnancies, especially among unmarried girls. This often condemns mother and child to poverty and frequently involves the child's grandparents. Education about responsibility seems to be one key to the prevention of such tragedy.

It seems appropriate at this point to review the status of fertility control in the 1990s. It is known that in the course of a year, 85

149

percent of sexually active women will become pregnant if they do not use any method of contraception. Use failure, sometimes known as typical use, refers to failure rates when use is not consistent or always correct. Method failure, sometimes known as perfect use, refers to failure rates for those whose use is consistent and always correct. In this discussion, failures refer to perfect use, without regard to convenience or preference. The figure given denotes the number of pregnancies per 100 women during one year of use.

Withdrawal—The failure rate is 4.0.

Condom—This protects against pregnancy and some sexually transmitted diseases. The sheath is made of latex or of animal tissue. The failure rate is 2.0.

Foam or suppository—The failure rate is 3.0.

Sponge—This is made of a soft, synthetic substance that contains a spermicide. Failure rate is 6.0 to 9.0. The higher rate is for the woman who has had a child.

Fertility awareness methods—These include the following: postovulatory 1.0; basal temperature 2.0; vaginal mucus 3.0; calendar 9.0. The numerals refer to the failure rate. These methods are more reliable when used together.

The following methods require consultation with a physician:

Pill—This is currently used by ten million women in the United States. Combination pills contain compounds similar to estrogen and progesterone. Mini pills contain only progesterone. The failure rates are respectively 0.1 and 0.5. A "morning-after" pill consists of a high dosage of hormones and is used only as an emergency measure.

IUD—More than 85 million women worldwide use this. It is a small plastic device that contains copper or a hormone. The failure rate for the copper type is 0.8 and for the hormone type 2.0.

Vasectomy—The operation blocks the vas deferens. The failure rate is 0.1.

Female sterilization—The fallopian tubes are closed off. The failure rate is 0.2.

Two contraceptives now approved by the Federal Drug Administration (FDA) will no doubt see increased use in this country. Both are highly effective.

Norplant—This is a long-standing (up to five years) contraceptive implant consisting of six nonbiodegradable silastic capsules containing the active drug. Experimental work is now in progress to produce degradable material that does not require removal.

Depo Provera—This long-acting contraceptive is injected into a muscle. To be effective, the injection is repeated every three months.

Some six million women in this country become pregnant every year. About half of these pregnancies are unintended. In some of these cases, induced abortion is apparently used as a method of birth control, although few people in the United States or Britain consider it a primary method of contraception. (Induced abortion differs from spontaneous abortion [miscarriage] when the embryo or fetus is expelled spontaneously from the uterus.)

More than 90 percent of all abortions are performed during the first three months of pregnancy. Done six to fourteen weeks after the last menstrual period, the suction curettage method is safer than childbirth. Second trimester abortions employ dilation of the cervix and subsequent evacuation of the uterine contents. The operation is done until the end of the 25th week. Abortions after the 24th week are performed only when there is a serious threat to the woman's life or if the fetus is severely deformed. A salt solution may be injected into the uterus to induce labor. Alternatively, injection of prostaglandin into the abdominal muscles causes the necessary uterine contractions and expulsion of the fetus.

A procedure called amniocentesis has affected the abortion rate. By analysis of the amniotic fluid of a fetus suspected of possessing, for example, a defective gene or a chromosomal disorder, such information can be confirmed, and the pregnancy terminated, if desired. The sex of the fetus can also be determined, and there have been cases where a fetus was aborted because it was not of the desired sex. (It was reported in 1991 that in India, where the female child is considered a liability, ultrasound testing of pregnant women has adversely affected the female/male population ratios.)

RU-486 (for Roussel-Uclaf, the French drug company that developed it) is an antiprogesterone drug created by Etienne-Emile Baulieu, professor of biochemistry at the University of Paris and head of research at Inserm, the French national health institute. The drug is effective as a postcoital contraceptive (morning-after pill) and in various medical conditions. When RU-486 is followed with a dose of synthetic hormone known as prostaglandin, it acts as an abortifacient up to five weeks after a missed period. RU-486 has been available in France since 1982. With the blessing of the Clinton administration, an effort is being made to have FDA approval so that it can be distributed for full use in the United States. The Right to Life movement strongly resists this as well as other drugs and methods that result in fetal death.

A number of contraceptives are in various stages of development. One is a vaccine intended to make a woman immune to sperm. Its inventor is John C. Herr of the University of Virginia, who will work in conjunction with Ortho Pharmaceutical Company. Other types of vaccines are in progress. A device that may become available soon is a female condom manufactured by Wisconsin Pharmacal. Vaginal rings that release hormones or hormonelike compounds have been developed abroad. Since these are inserted and removed by the user, they appear to be promising. Various ways to suppress sperm production have also been investigated. Transdermal patches to deliver hormones are also under consideration, and blocking ovulation in some way other than the pill is a possibility. The list goes on, but research is costly.

The abortion issue is involved in this research. The Helms Amendment of 1973 forbids funding research on compounds that act after fertilization. The Agency for International Development defines pregnancy as fertilization, making such U.S. aid illegal. The National Institutes of Health, on the other hand, define pregnancy as implantation, but the law also prevents NIH study of methods designed to cause an abortion and also study of contraception that interferes with implantation. Feminists have high hopes that the Clinton administration will act to clear up this confusion and create a climate more conducive to contraceptive research.

Planned Parenthood Federation of America is the nation's oldest and largest voluntary reproductive health care organization. It is dedicated to the principle that every individual has a fundamental right to choose when or whether to have children. This federation of more than 170 not-for-profit corporations, operating more than 900 clinics in 40 states and the District of Columbia, meets the family planning needs of nearly four million Americans each year. This includes the provision of contraception, abortion, sterilization, and fertility services. Relevant biomedical, socioeconomic, and demographic research is encouraged. Through its international program, Planned Parenthood helps to meet the family planning needs of women and men in the developing world.

Some comparison of the women discussed in the preceding pages might be useful to our greater understanding of their accomplishments. We can learn much from both the negative and the positive aspects of their lives, and we can make a few generalizations.

So far as economics and opportunity are concerned, Fanny Wright, Kate McCormick, and Mary Calderone came from families of privilege. Annie Besant, Marie Stopes, Mary Dennett, Betty Friedan, Virginia Johnson, and Sarah Weddington lived comfortably when they were growing up. Emma Goldman and, to a lesser extent, Margaret Sanger saw some deprivation, but neither was destitute.

Each woman received at least some education; all had intellectual gifts and sought knowledge for pleasure as well as for practical reasons. Annie Besant would have liked additional formal learning, and the same can probably be said for Emma Goldman and Margaret Sanger. Ironically, Emma Goldman actually had the opportunity to become a physician, but she found that other matters were more important to her at that time. Marie Stopes showed rare determination in obtaining the university training she desired. Mary Calderone, Betty Friedan, Sarah Weddington, and Virginia Johnson obtained advanced education.

Parental guidance and influence were strong in the lives of Margaret Sanger, Marie Stopes, and Mary Calderone, whose fathers in particular were important to them. The relationship between Emma Goldman and her parents was a poor one, but she was blessed by the care and devotion of a sister. Fanny Wright, left an orphan, possibly considered Lafayette the father she never knew.

Religion is the keynote in the lives of many reformers and activists—Harriet Beecher Stowe immediately comes to mind—but most of the women considered here showed surprisingly little interest in religion, with two exceptions. Sarah Weddington is the daughter of a Methodist minister. Mary Calderone, in discussing criticism she received because of her stance on sexuality education, declared that it was her Quaker faith that sustained her when "terrible things were said." Margaret Sanger had a devout mother who exposed her children to the tenets of Catholicism, over the objections of her atheist husband, Michael Higgins. As Sanger's adult activities caused more and more confrontation with the Catholic church, she developed a distrust and hatred of it. Marie Stopes, with a Protestant mother, had the same distrust.

Motivation looms large in directing one's activities. Emma Goldman's life exemplifies adherence to an ideal, in this case anarchism. Her performance showed unusual courage, albeit in quest of impractical goals. Motivated by her ideal, which was the advancement of women, Katharine McCormick, after much study, donated millions to causes she deemed worthy. Humanitarian instincts drove Margaret Sanger. At the same time, she was also intensely ambitious and sometimes not disposed to give credit where it was due. Marie Stopes's admirable efforts on behalf of sex education and birth control were spoiled by her egotism, which became more and more difficult to deal with.

Annie Besant intended to improve the lot of humanity, and the Bradlaugh-Besant case insured that contraceptive information could not be suppressed. Beyond that issue and the publication of her *The Law of Population*, her varied efforts in other fields seem to have been too diffuse to be really productive.

Character and personality traits deserve mention. As noted, Goldman showed courage on numerous occasions. Sanger, Besant, and Dennett also faced arrest without flinching. When Calderone advocated teaching youngsters about human sexuality, her effort was denounced as "a Communist plot to overthrow the United States." Nevertheless, she stood firm against such unfair criticism. Frances Wright had sufficient confidence in her vision for Nashoba to attempt to implement it. Bad luck and bad advice contributed to her failure, but the fact that she tried such a venture is remarkable. Her plans for public education were progressive, and she did not fail to make them known. Women seldom spoke in public, but Wright, Besant, and Goldman did not hesitate to lecture because they knew they could do it well. In fact, all 11 women were aggressive enough to try the unusual. Flexibility is a desirable characteristic that Sanger, Friedan, Stopes, and Johnson used to advantage; Dennett appeared less flexible than these women. Compassion is reflected in the devotion to pacificism advocated by Goldman, Dennett, Sanger, and Calderone.

According to Calvin Coolidge, the trait of perseverance is essential to an individual with a mission:

> Nothing in this world can take the place of persistence. Talent will not; nothing is more common than unsuccessful people with talent. Genius will not; unrewarded genius is almost a proverb. Education will not; the world is full of educated derelicts. Persistence and determination alone are omnipotent. The slogan "press on" has solved and always will solve the problems of the human race.

Margaret Sanger had a vision that there could be equality for women in matters of sexuality and reproduction. Her sustained persistence in working towards that goal bears out Coolidge's contention.

Though she was dedicated to women's rights, Betty Friedan urged cooperation between the sexes instead of dissent. Despite her individuality, Frances Wright worked well with Robert Dale Owen. Annie Besant, certainly an independent woman, had a good working relationship with Charles Bradlaugh. Emma Goldman and Ben Reitman worked effectively together in promoting contraception. Early in her career at least, Marie Stopes accepted her husband's advice and financial backing for her movement. The working partnership between William Masters and Virginia Johnson was very strong; one seemed to complement the other. Margaret Sanger, on the other hand, showed little interest in forming a professional union with William Sanger, although he was a strong advocate of birth control. Noah Slee, her second husband, helped her with advice and money, but she did not seem eager to make him a real part of her cause.

Shakespeare reminds us of the tide in human affairs that taken at the flood leads to success. Politicians, reformers, and others have always put much emphasis on the "right time" to launch a campaign. Some of these women were adept at seizing opportunities that arose. Marie Stopes as the author of the popular *Married Love* was in a good position to popularize birth control; Betty Friedan recognized that women of the post–World War II era were ready for changes that she envisioned; Kate McCormick was convinced that the time for an oral contraceptive was at hand; Sarah Weddington and her friends sensed that abortion reform might have a chance in the 1970s; Virginia Johnson saw how new information about sexual dysfunction could be used innovatively to create improvement.

Marriage and children have a profound effect on a woman's life. Of the 11 women, all but McCormick were divorced, some of them more than once. All but Goldman, McCormick, and Weddington had children. If Dennett had been childless, it is unlikely that her famous pamphlet and the book about it would even have been written. Likewise, had Stopes had a satisfying first marriage, probably *Married Love* would not have appeared. Having to support her children no doubt made Friedan more sensitive to some of the problems of a single mother. Wright's marriage appears to have been a disaster; she became estranged from both her husband and her only child. Not only was her personal life unhappy, but her work for various reforms seems to have had little meaning for her.

Did these women retain their enthusiasm for the cause of women's reproductive rights as they grew older? Virginia Johnson continues to write in her field; Mary Calderone has been productive; Betty Friedan brings to the problems of aging some of the insight she had for the problems of women. The supreme example is Margaret Sanger, who remained devoted to her ideals throughout retirement and old age.

There are important individual differences, but these women had something significant in common. Although none of them knew real poverty or a continuing intolerable existence, each desired a better world for others and herself. And each set out to obtain that world. Above all, they were not inhibited from reaching their goals by the restrictions set on women of their day.

Bibliography

General

Ackernecht, Erwin H. *A Short History of Medicine.* Rev. ed. Baltimore: Johns Hopkins University Press, 1982.

Barker-Benfield, G. J. *The Horrors of the Half-Known Life: Male Attitudes Toward Women and Sexuality in Nineteenth-Century America.* New York: Harper & Row, 1976.

Barret-Ducrocq, Francoise. *Love in the Time of Victoria: Sexuality and Desire Among Working-Class Men and Women in Nineteenth-Century London.* New York: Viking, 1992.

Costello, John. *Virtue Under Fire: How WWII Changed Our Social and Sexual Attitudes.* Boston: Little, Brown, 1985.

Fryer, Peter. *The Birth Controllers.* New York: Stein and Day, 1965.

Gordon, Linda. *Woman's Body, Woman's Right: A Social History of Birth Control in America.* New York: Grossman, 1976.

Gruver, Rebecca Brooks. *An American History.* 4th ed. 2 vols. New York: Newbery Award Records, 1985.

Hartman, Carl G. *Science and the Safe Period.* Baltimore: Williams & Wilkins, 1962.

Himes, Norman E. *Medical History of Contraception.* 1936. Reprint. New York: Gamut, 1963.

Jacobs, Aletta H. *Herinneringen.* Amsterdam: Van Holkema and Warendorf, 1924.

McHenry, Robert, ed. *Famous American Women: A Biographical Dictionary from Colonial Times to the Present.* New York: Dover, 1983. (Originally published as *Liberty's Women*, 1980.)

McLaren, Angus. *A History of Contraception: From Antiquity to the Present Day.* Cambridge, Mass.: Basil Blackwell, 1990.

McLaughlin, Steven D. *The Changing Lives of American Women.* Chapel Hill: University of North Carolina Press, 1988.

Miles, Rosalind. *A Women's History of the World.* (First American edition.) Topsfield, Mass.: Salem House, 1989.

Petrie, Glen. *A Singular Iniquity: The Campaigns of Josephine Butler.* New York: Viking, 1971.

Reed, James. *From Private Vice to Public Virtue: The Birth Control Movement and American Society Since 1930.* 1978. Reprint. Princeton, N.J.: Princeton University Press, 1983.

Riddle, John M. *Contraception and Abortion from Ancient Times to the Renaissance.* Cambridge: Harvard University Press, 1992.

Scott, George R. *Ladies of Vice: A History of Prostitution from Antiquity to the Present Day.* London: Tallis Press, 1968.

Spurlock, John C. *Free Love: Marriage and Middle-Class Radicalism in America , 1825–1860.* New York: New York University Press, 1988.

Wood, Clive, and Beryl Suitters. *The Fight for Acceptance: The History of Contraception.* Aylesbury, U.K.: Medical and Technical Publishing, 1970.

Frances Wright

D'Arusmont, Frances Wright. *Life, Letters, and Lectures, 1834–1844.* Reprint. New York: Arno Press, 1972.

Eckhardt, Celia Morris. *Fanny Wright: Rebel in America.* Cambridge: Harvard University Press, 1984.

Leopold, Richard William. *Robert Dale Owen: A Biography.* Cambridge: Harvard University Press, 1940.

Owen, Robert Dale. *Moral Physiology; or A Brief and Plain Treatise on the Population Question.* 10th ed. Boston: J. P. Mendum, 1875.

Pancoast, Elinor, and Anne E. Lincoln. *The Incorrigible Idealist: Robert Dale Owen in America.* Bloomingdale, Ind.: Principia, 1940.

Perkins, Alice J. G., and Theresa Wolfson. *Frances Wright, Free Enquirer: The Story of a Temperament.* New York: Harper & Brothers, 1939.

Rothman, David J., and Sheila M. Rothman, eds. *Birth Control and Morality in Nineteenth-Century America: Two Dimensions (FRUITS OF PHILOSOPHY and MORAL PHILOSOPHY).* New York: Arno Press, 1972.

Waterman, William Randall. *Frances Wright.* New York: Columbia University Press, 1924.

Wright, Frances. *Course of Popular Lectures.* New York: Free Enquirer, 1829.

Annie Besant

Besant, Annie. *An Autobiography.* Philadelphia: Henry Altemus, 1893.

Besterman, Theodore. *Mrs. Annie Besant: A Modern Prophet.* London: Kegan Paul, Trench, Trubner, 1934.

Chandrasekhar, Sripati. *"A Dirty, Filthy Book": The Writings of Charles Knowlton and Annie Besant on Reproductive Physiology and Birth Control and an Account of the Bradlaugh-Besant Trial.* Berkeley: University of California Press, 1981.

Mill, John Stuart. *The Subjection of Women.* 1869. Reprint. Cambridge: MIT Press, 1970.

Nethercot, Arthur H. *The Last Four Lives of Annie Besant.* Chicago: University of Chicago Press, 1963.

Tribe, David. *President Charles Bradlaugh, M.P.* Hamden, Conn.: Archon Books, 1971. (Originally published in Great Britain by Elek Books.)

Emma Goldman

Bonner, Thomas Neville. *To the Ends of the Earth: Women's Search for Education in Medicine.* Cambridge: Harvard University Press, 1992.

Broun, Heywood, and Margaret Leech. *Anthony Comstock: Roundsman of the Lord.* New York: Boni, 1927.

Chalberg, John. *Emma Goldman: American Individualist.* New York: Harper-Collins, 1991.

Comstock, Anthony. *Frauds Exposed: How the People Are Deceived and Robbed, and Youth Corrupted.* 1880. Reprint. Montclair, N.J.: Paterson Smith, 1969.

Drinnon, Richard. *Rebel in Paradise: A Biography of Emma Goldman.* 1961. Reprint. New York: Harper & Row, 1976.

Goldman, Emma. *Living My Life.* New York: Alfred A. Knopf, 1931.

Morton, Marian J. *Emma Goldman and the American Left: "Nowhere at Home."* New York: Twayne, 1992.

Wexler, Alice. *Emma Goldman: An Intimate Life.* New York: Pantheon, 1984.

Margaret Sanger

Caldwell, Mark. *The Last Crusade: The War on Consumption, 1882–1954.* New York: Atheneum, 1988.

Chesler, Ellen. *Woman of Valor: Margaret Sanger and the Birth Control Movement in America.* New York: Simon and Schuster, 1992.

Douglas, Emily Taft. *Margaret Sanger: Pioneer of the Future.* New York: Holt, 1970.

Gray, Madeline. *Margaret Sanger: A Biography of the Champion of Birth Control.* New York: Marek, 1978.

Sanger, Margaret. *An Autobiography.* New York: Norton, 1938.

————. *My Fight for Birth Control.* 1931. Reprint. Elmsford, N.Y.: Maxwell Reprint Co., 1969.

Marie Stopes

Hall, Ruth. *Passionate Crusader: The Life of Marie Stopes.* New York: Harcourt Brace Jovanovich, 1977.

Marie Stopes Clinic. *Your Body. A Woman's Guide to Her Sexual Health.* Wellingsborough, Northamptonshire, U.K.: Thorsons Publishing, 1987.

Maude, Almer. *Marie Stopes: Her Work and Play.* New York: G. P. Putnam's Sons, 1933.

Rose, June. *Marie Stopes and the Sexual Revolution.* London: Faber & Faber, 1992.

Stopes, Marie Carmichael. *Married Love.* 1918. Reprint. London: G. P. Putnam's Sons, 1931.

————. *Contraception: Its Theory, History and Practice. A Manual for the Medical and Legal Professions.* London: Bale and Danielsson, 1925.

Mary Dennett

Dennett, Mary Ware. *Birth Control Laws: Shall We Keep Them or Change Them or Abolish Them?* New York: Frederick H. Hitchcock, 1926.

————. *Who's Obscene?* New York: Vanguard, 1930.

Lash, Christopher. *Notable American Women, 1607–1950.* Vol. 1, edited by Edward T. Jones et al., 463–65. Cambridge, Mass.: Belknap, 1971.

Lee, Erma Conkling, ed. *The Biographical Cyclopaedia of American Women.* Vol. 2, 236–40. New York: Franklin W. Lee, 1925.

Sanger, Margaret. *An Autobiography.* New York: Norton, 1938.

Mary Calderone

Calderone, Mary Steichen, ed. *Abortion in the United States: Report of a Conference Sponsored by the Planned Parenthood Federation of America.* New York: Hoeber-Harper, 1958.

Calderone, Mary, and Eric Johnson. *The Family Book About Sexuality.* Rev. ed. New York: Harper & Row, 1989.

Moritz, Charles, ed. *Current Biography.* 53–56. Bronx, N.Y.: H. W. Wilson, 1967.

Sullivan, Mary. *Contemporary Authors.* Vol. 104, edited by Frances C. Lochen, 68–70. Detroit: Gale Research, 1982.

Westheimer, Ruth. *Dr. Ruth's Guide to Good Sex.* New York: Warner, 1983.

Katharine McCormick

Bemis, William H., et al. *A Tribute to Katharine Dexter McCormick.* Comments delivered at MIT, Cambridge, March 1, 1968.

Davis, Kenneth. "The Story of the Pill." *American Heritage* 29, no. 5 (August-September, 1978): 80–90.

Maisel, Albert Q. *The Hormone Quest.* New York: Random House, 1965.

Pincus, Gregory. *The Control of Fertility.* New York: Academic Press, 1965.

Reed, James. *Notable American Women: The Modern Period.* Edited by Barbara Sickerman and Carol Green. 440–42. Cambridge, Mass.: Belknap, 1980.

Riddle, John M., and J. Worth Estes. "Oral Contraceptives in Ancient and Medieval Times." *American Scientist* Vol. 80, #3 (May-June 1992): 226–33.

Friedan, Betty

Carlson, Elliot, and Susan L. Crowley. "The Friedan Mystique." *AARP Bulletin* Vol. 33, #8 (September 1992): 18.

Davis, Flora. *Moving the Mountain: The Women's Movement in America Since 1960.* New York: Simon and Schuster, 1991.

Friedan, Betty. *The Feminine Mystique.* New York: Norton, 1963.

_____. *It Changed My Life: Writings on the Women's Movement.* 1976. Reprint. New York: Norton, 1985.

_____. *The Second Stage.* 1981. Reprint. Rev. ed. New York: Summit Books, 1986.

Moritz, Charles, ed. *Current Biography Yearbook.* 188–92. Bronx, N.Y.: H. W. Wilson, 1989.

Sarah Weddington

Baird, Robert M., and Stuart E. Rosenbaum. *The Ethics of Abortion: Pro-Life vs. Pro-Choice.* Buffalo, N.Y.: Prometheus, 1989.

Drucker, Dan. *Abortion Decisions of the Supreme Court, 1973 through 1989: A Comprehensive Review with Historical Commentary.* Jefferson, N.C.: McFarland, 1990.

Podell, Janet, ed. *The Reference Shelf.* Vol. 62, #4. New York: H. W. Wilson, 1960.

Rosenblatt, Roger. *Life Itself: Abortion in the American Mind.* New York: Random House, 1990.

Tribe, Lawrence. *Abortion: The Clash of Absolutes.* New York: Norton, 1990.

Weddington, Sarah. *A Question of Choice.* New York: G. P. Putnam's Sons, 1992.

Wennberg, Robert. *Life in the Balance: Exploring the Abortion Controversy.* Grand Rapids, Mich.: Eerdmans, 1985.

Virginia Johnson

Baulieu, Etienne-Emile, with Mort Rosenblum. *The "Abortion Pill."* New York: Simon and Schuster, 1990.

Crane, Margaret. "A Life in the Day of Virginia Masters." *Seen* (February 1993): 10–11.

Holloway, Marguerite. "Obstacle Course." *Scientific American* Vol. 268, #4 (April 1993): 18, 22–23.

Janus, Samuel, and Cynthia Janus. *Janus Report on Sexual Behavior.* New York: Wiley, 1993.

Masters, William H., and Virginia E. Johnson. *Human Sexual Inadequacy.* Boston: Little, Brown, 1970.

————, and Virginia E. Johnson. *Human Sexual Response.* Boston: Little, Brown, 1966.

Masters, William H., et al. *Crisis: Heterosexual Behavior in the Age of AIDS.* New York: Grove, 1988.

_____. *The Pleasure Bond: A New Look at Sexuality and Commitment.* Boston: Little, Brown, 1975.

Mortiz, Charles, ed. *Current Biography Yearbook.* 198–201. Bronx, N.Y.: H. W. Wilson, 1976.

Planned Parenthood Federation of America. *Abortion: Questions and Answers.* (Flyer.) New York, 1991.

_____. *Facts About Birth Control.* (Flyer.) New York, 1992.
_____. *You and the Pill.* (Flyer.) New York, 1987.

Index

Numbers in **boldface** refer to pages with photographs.

167